EXECUTIVE FUNCTIONS AT HOME AND SCHOOL

SIX SKILLS YOUNG LEARNERS NEED TO SUCCEED

Christina Young, M.S.Ed., LPC
with Christina Nichols, Ph.D.

Foreword by Edward M. Hallowell, M.D.

EXECUTIVE FUNCTIONS AT HOME AND SCHOOL:
SIX SKILLS YOUNG LEARNERS NEED TO SUCCEED

by Christina Young, M.S.Ed., LPC
with Christina Nichols, Ph.D.

All rights reserved. Except as indicated, no part of this book may be reproduced, transmitted in any form by any means, electronic or mechanical, including photocopying, recording, or by any information storage and retrieval system, without permission in writing from the publisher. For information regarding permissions, contact pressed@plussed.org.

PLUSSED· Pressed, LLC
Bronx, NY 10471
www.plussed.org/plussed-pressed

© 2017 Christina Young
Design by Atelier Cho Thompson *in collaboration* with the boxed cloud
Illustrations by Atelier Cho Thompson

ISBN: 978-0-9986791-0-5
Printed in the United States of America
1 2 3 4 5 6   22 21 20 19 18 17

Thank you to our colleagues, young learners, and families at Riverdale Country School, Horace Mann School, and Hallowell Center. For their support of this book, we want to acknowledge: Dominic A.A. Randolph, Kelley Nicholson-Flynn, Milton Sipp, Kevin Mattingly, and Jed Silverstein at Riverdale Country School; Thomas M. Kelly at Horace Mann School; and Edward M. Hallowell and Sue Hallowell at Hallowell Center.

TABLE OF CONTENTS

Foreword 1

Introduction 2
    What Makes This the Book for You? 2
    How to Use This Book 4

Chapter 1: Six Key Executive Function Skills for Young Learners 5
    Overview of the Six Key Executive Function Skill Sets
        for Young Learners 6
    What You Need to Know about the Prefrontal Cortex and
        the Amygdala 8
    Who Needs Help Building Stronger Executive Functions? .. 10
        Resource Sheet: Key Executive Function Skill Sets
            for Young Learners 13

Chapter 2: What You Need to Know about Mindfulness,
    Character Strengths, and a Growth Mindset 15
    Mindfulness and Executive Functions 15
        Vignette: Catch Your Breath 17
    Character Strengths and Executive Functions 18
    Character Strengths 19
        Resource Sheet: Overlap of Character Strengths and
            Executive Functions 25
    Growth Mindset and Executive Functions 26
    The Foundations of Active Learning 29
    The Myth of Multitasking 32

Chapter 3: What Makes All of This So Important? 35
    A Strengths and Skills Approach 35
    ADHD and Other Learning Differences 37
    Psychoeducational Evaluation 37

Chapter 4: What's Important to Know about Memory and Attention? 41
- Memory 41
- Attention 45

Chapter 5: How Executive Function Challenges Look at Home and School 49
- 1. Organize 49
  - *Vignette: Time and Material Management* 50
- 2. Prioritize 52
  - *Vignette: Planning* 55
  - *Vignette: Seeing the Forest for the Trees* 57
- 3. Take Action! 59
  - *Vignette: Perfectionism* 60
- 4. Reflect 63
  - *Vignette: Flexibility* 64
- 5. Balance—Part I: Emotional Regulation 66
- 6. Balance—Part II: Emotional Modulation 67
  - *Vignette: The Battle of Everything* 68

Chapter 6: How to Partner with Young Learners to Teach Executive Function Skills 73
- What Is a Coach Approach? 73
- Why Try a Coach Approach? 74
- Working with a Professional Coach 74
- Using a Coach Approach at Home or School 75
- The Benefits of Using a Coach Approach 76
  - *Vignette: Speak to Me after Class* 78

Chapter 7: Tools to Teach Executive Function Skills at Home .. 81
- Helping Your Child Set Effective Goals 81
- Strategies to Organize and Prioritize 81

    Strategies to Take Action!...................................87
    Strategies to Reflect and Balance.........................88
        Vignette: Balance *89*
    Strategies to Practice Mindfulness.......................90
        Worksheet: Family Self-Assessment *95*

Chapter 8: Tools to Teach Executive Function Skills at School..97
    Helping Your Students Set Effective Goals................97
    Strategies for Organization 98
    Sample Student Monthly Calendar......................101
    Strategies to Prioritize 102
        Resource Sheet: Two-Column Notes *107*
    Strategies to Take Action!...............................108
        Resource Sheet: Active Study Strategies................. *111*
        Worksheet: Pretest Self-Reflection *113*
    Strategies to Reflect................................... 114
        Resource Sheet: Reflection Exercises *117*
        Worksheet: Note Taking Reflection.................... *119*
        Resource Sheet: Error Analysis for Math *121*
    Strategies to Balance...................................122
        Worksheet: Reflection — Express Yourself!............. *125*
    Strategies to Practice Mindfulness......................126
        Resource Sheet: Skills for Student Success............. *133*

Conclusion: Putting It All Together 135

References 141

About the Author 145

Contributors..147

FOREWORD

"We all know that children don't come with manuals ... but this is a great manual for parents and teachers who want to understand the children in their lives!"

—Edward M. Hallowell

Between the ages of 11 and 21, our beloved children can at times seem impossible to understand—or just impossible. How often have you thought, or said, or yelled something along the lines of, "How could you forget? I must have told you a hundred times!" or "This is the third time I've come in here to wake you up!" or "What were you thinking?"

Parenting and teaching are huge jobs filled with day-to-day challenges. Parents and teachers deserve help. Help that is easy to access. Help that saves time and stops power struggles. Help that doesn't collect dust sitting on your bedside table, waiting until you have time to read it. This book helps.

There are many books out there that tell you *what* to do to help your children get organized, manage their time, and get to work. In eight short chapters, this book will fill you in on *why* those skills are so important and *how* you can help teens get better at them. Understanding the most important skills for young learners will help you step back and see the big picture—one of the very skills our children need to learn!

What sets this book apart from other books on executive functions? First, it gets right to the points that matter most for parents and teachers. It's easy to read and easy to relate to your children. Second, it focuses on skills that can be taught and strengths that can be developed. Understanding how to cultivate those skills and strengths over time is far more important than any prescribed routine or list of tasks. Finally, it always keeps the most important thing front and center: your relationship with the children in your life.

Academic challenges will come and go, but strong personal connections, skills, and strengths will last a lifetime.

Edward M. Hallowell, M.D.
Child and Adult Psychiatrist
Founder of Hallowell Center

INTRODUCTION

WHAT MAKES THIS THE BOOK FOR YOU?

We know how busy life can get. Short and practical, this book is designed to give you information and resources to help the young learners in your lives. Aimed at the pivotal middle and high school years, the information and strategies also apply to elementary school students and young adults.

There are a lot of books out there about executive functions. This one clearly and concisely defines the most important executive function skills for young learners and shows what makes them so important.

If you already know why executive function skills are vitally important, we illustrate the relationship between those skills and mindfulness, character strengths, and a growth mindset. This whole-child approach is far more effective than focusing on the skills alone, and it sets our book apart from the others.

We know young learners often work ineffectively, and it is hard to teach effective work habits. Effective work requires strong executive function skills. This book outlines the foundations of active—and effective—learning and includes home and classroom strategies.

We pulled together the research, information, and tools we've used over the years. We then pared it down to what we believe will be the most essential, relevant, and useful for you. You will find vignettes throughout the book that illustrate how executive function challenges look at home and at school—and how to help. We don't want this book to end up half-read on a shelf—we want dog-eared pages and notes in the margins!

Chapter 1 defines six key executive function skill sets for young learners. It dips into neuroscience to highlight the important roles played by the amygdala and the prefrontal cortex.

Chapter 2 explores the relationship among executive function skills, mindfulness, and character strengths—each a leg of the three-legged stool that supports a balanced young learner. A growth mindset takes that foundation and helps children thrive. This chapter also reviews the foundations of active learning.

Chapter 3 discusses the benefits of a strengths-based approach to working with young learners. It discusses the impact of learning differences on executive function skills and provides an overview of the benefits and components of psychoeducational testing.

Chapter 4 provides an overview of memory and attention—critical components of all executive function skills. Challenges with working memory and attention are often misread as "not caring" or "not trying." Identifying underlying challenges is important for successful intervention.

Chapter 5 goes more deeply into each executive function skill set and ties in the main ideas throughout the book. It includes the components of setting successful short-term goals. This chapter features several vignettes that illustrate common executive function challenges, followed by strategies to address those challenges.

Chapter 6 discusses how to partner with young learners by using a coach approach to develop stronger executive function skills while cultivating mindfulness, character strengths, and a growth mindset. Those skills and strengths will help young learners gain independence through responsible actions and healthy decisions while strengthening parent–child and teacher–student relationships.

Chapter 7 provides an overview of strategies for parents to strengthen their child's executive function skills at home. The information and context from the first six chapters are vital to implementing these strategies successfully.

Chapter 8 provides strategies and resources geared for teachers to teach these skills in the classroom. The information and context from the first six chapters are vital to implementing these strategies successfully. Many of the strategies are for middle and high school classrooms, but they can be adapted for younger and older learners.

HOW TO USE THIS BOOK

Take Note
Each chapter includes space in the margins to note your comments, questions, and ideas. We've also included full-page Take Note pages for your use.

What's the Big Picture?
Each chapter ends with a short summary or main takeaways to review the big picture and connect one chapter to another.

Now What?
Each chapter includes questions designed to help you put the information to use. Some chapters include recommendations after the questions.

Use the Now What? questions to connect what you've read to the young learners in your life.

Resource Sheets and Worksheets
Throughout the book, you will find resource sheets that provide a big-picture overview of the material and worksheets for use at home or school.

CHAPTER 1 | KEY SKILLS | MINDSET | SO WHAT? | MEMORY | CHALLENGES | PARTNERING | TOOLS AT HOME | TOOLS AT SCHOOL

1 SIX KEY EXECUTIVE FUNCTION SKILLS FOR YOUNG LEARNERS

VIGNETTE

Charlotte, a 12-year-old girl, slammed her door, put in her earphones, and picked up her phone. Her mom yelled after her and then sat at the kitchen table to reread the academic note. Charlotte had always done well in school without much stress at home. But in the first semester of seventh grade, she received two academic notes from history and two from science. The notes reiterated the concerns that teachers in several subjects shared at the parent–teacher conference: Charlotte did not consistently turn in homework assignments; her work seemed rushed; and while she seemed to understand the concepts, her performance on tests did not represent that knowledge. Each night at home had become a battle. Charlotte was irritable and defensive when her mom tried to review the night's assignments or the class websites. Her mom resented having to micromanage each night's work, but she thought it was the only way to make sure that Charlotte completed it. The tension between the two of them was growing, and Charlotte's work was not improving. Instead, Charlotte blamed her teachers, her classes, and even her mom for her missed assignments and errors. Charlotte's mom had tried everything she could think of to beg, bribe, or convince Charlotte to "pay attention" to her assignments and "work harder." She didn't know what else to do.

This vignette is just one example of how executive function challenges can look at home. **Executive functions** is an umbrella term for the management of cognitive processes. They are the chief executive officer of the brain[1]: responsible for seeing the big picture, solving problems, delegating resources, and reviewing the outcome.

Starting in sixth and seventh grades, the academic expectations for students begin to shift. From middle school through high school, students are expected to take on more and more responsibility for their daily, weekly, and semester schedules and workloads. Longer-term projects and papers require sustained effort over time. Students review their work independently and create their own study strategies for quizzes and tests. Perhaps most challenging, students are expected to connect new information to prior or background knowledge, differentiate main ideas from supporting details, understand facts and events from different perspectives, and form opinions backed up with evidence from the text that they share verbally or in writing.

Asking students to "work harder" does not help them meet these challenges. Young learners must learn how to work more effectively. That means learning active study strategies and committing to routines that support organization, planning, prioritization, and motivation.

On top of the increased academic workload, young learners are managing social and emotional challenges. More co-curricular events and social events take up time in the evenings and on weekends. Preteens and teens are also experiencing physical and emotional challenges related to puberty that can trigger strong emotional responses.

To meet the new challenges of seventh grade, Charlotte needs stronger skills to manage her time, organize, prioritize, and reflect—several of the key executive function skill sets at the center of this book. She will also benefit from stronger emotional regulation and modulation skills to support her through the hard, uncertain work of learning.

Here is a brief introduction to the six key executive function skill sets that young learners need to succeed. We will discuss each skill set in depth in Chapter 5.

OVERVIEW OF THE SIX KEY EXECUTIVE FUNCTION SKILL SETS FOR YOUNG LEARNERS

1. ORGANIZE

This skill set includes time management, material management, and a sense of time. This is the most concrete skill set, so it's a great place to start building stronger executive function skills. Organization includes the ability to remain aware of daily tasks and the bigger picture—the weekly and monthly schedule. It supports all the other skill sets. We include healthy sleep routines, nutrition, and exercise in this foundational skill set, because they affect every aspect of learning and wellbeing.

2. PRIORITIZE

This is choosing what to tackle first, second, and third. This skill set includes how to plan, solve problems, and manage busy school and co-curricular schedules. Critical-thinking skills require the ability to prioritize information in order to identify main ideas and form academic arguments.

3. TAKE ACTION!

Activation is the ability to get started on a task. This skill set includes tackling procrastination, using external motivation, cultivating internal motivation, and identifying the purpose of tasks. It includes focus—or sustained attention to the task at hand.

4. REFLECT

Reflection involves connecting new knowledge to background knowledge, synthesizing information and input from many different sources, and articulating one's own interpretation or ideas.

Academic reflection requires metacognition—or "thinking about thinking"—and an awareness of one's personal learning strengths and challenges. It's how students connect the dots between the big picture—the concept or main ideas—and the supporting details. It helps students articulate their own ideas and arguments. Academic reflection builds **cognitive flexibility**—the ability to understand events or ideas from different perspectives as well as change one's strategy or approach to a task.

Personal reflection allows a young learner to understand what they are thinking and feeling. It includes self-awareness and supports metacognition and cognitive flexibility, especially the ability to understand events and ideas from different perspectives. Young learners who have the ability to reflect meaningfully are better able to manage stress, identify effective study strategies, and understand their external and internal motivators.

TAKE NOTE

5. BALANCE—PART I: EMOTIONAL REGULATION

Emotional regulation is the skill of acknowledging and balancing strong emotions when they arise. This skill set includes impulse control and stress management.

6. BALANCE—PART II: EMOTIONAL MODULATION

Emotional modulation is the skill of expressing feelings at an appropriate volume and at an appropriate time, especially when strong emotions arise. Many social emotional learning programs are geared toward strengthening emotional regulation and modulation skills through active listening, effective communication, and conflict resolution.

What makes these all of these skills so challenging for teens? Human development!

WHAT YOU NEED TO KNOW ABOUT THE PREFRONTAL CORTEX AND THE AMYGDALA

The **prefrontal cortex** is the region of the brain that primarily controls executive functions and gives us the capacity to exercise "good judgment" when presented with difficult life situations. But the prefrontal cortex is not fully developed until the mid-20s—this is why adolescence is defined up to age 25.[2] The prefrontal cortex takes in information and applies reason, problem solving, and other critical-thinking skills to determine and achieve specific goals.

The brain region that houses our strongest emotions—including fear, anger, and joy—is the limbic system, specifically a region called the **amygdala** (pronounced uh-MIG-duh-luh). Unlike the prefrontal cortex, the amygdala is largely developed at birth. Here's an important fact for anyone parenting or teaching young learners: An adolescent's amygdala is larger than an adult's amygdala.

| CHAPTER 1 KEY SKILLS | MINDSET | SO WHAT? | MEMORY | CHALLENGES | PARTNERING | TOOLS AT HOME | TOOLS AT SCHOOL |

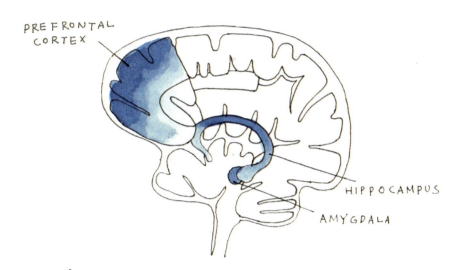

That suggests that adolescents actually experience emotions more powerfully than adults, but they don't have a fully developed prefrontal cortex to help them cope with those emotions and choose the best response.[3]

Based on the strong emotions they experience, young learners may act—or, more accurately, react—without planning before or reflecting afterward. In order to have the ability to *choose* how to best respond to a challenge in the moment it arises, young learners need to practice identifying and coping with their initial emotional reaction before intentionally acting in a way that best supports their wellbeing and goals. That is one of the foundational skills that we identify as **mindfulness**. (Chapter 2 discusses this in depth.)

Mindfulness skills combined with stronger executive function skills help young learners be more independent, responsible, and successful. When young learners connect the mindfulness skills and executive function skills they apply to the increased success they experience, they will also strengthen motivation and resilience.

WHO NEEDS HELP BUILDING STRONGER EXECUTIVE FUNCTIONS?

Based on what we know about how the human brain develops, we can expect that *every* young learner needs help cultivating strong executive function skills that support academic and personal success. Strong executive function skills allow young learners to work independently, cope with challenges in responsible and healthy ways, and work to their full potential.

Neuroscientist Adele Diamond's research shows that the prefrontal cortex and executive functions are negatively affected by stress, sadness, loneliness, and a lack of physical fitness.[4] Focusing solely on academic skills and academic performance will not be effective without considering young learners' wellbeing—including social, emotional, and physical health.

Many schools provide tools to support executive function skills, such as a school planner. But they are often used ineffectively—or not used at all—by students who do not understand how these tools can help strengthen their own individual skills. Understanding how key executive function skills support performance and wellbeing will help you communicate the benefits of using the strategies described in this book.

WHAT'S THE BIG PICTURE?

"Working harder" doesn't work. It's not about working harder, but working more *effectively*. All young learners need help to develop the skills they need to work effectively as academic demands change, reflect on the results of their actions and change strategies as needed, and balance strong emotions in healthy and productive ways.

NOW WHAT?

- Help the young learners in your life identify their specific, skill-based strengths and challenges.
- The following chapters include information on targeting and strengthening specific skills and setting realistic, motivating goals.

Think of a few young learners in your life. What are their specific skill-based strengths and challenges?

The following summary of the Six Key Executive Function Skill Sets for Young Learners references character strengths. We discuss character strengths in Chapter 2.

TAKE NOTE

KEY EXECUTIVE FUNCTION SKILL SETS FOR YOUNG LEARNERS

ORGANIZE
- Time and material management and sense of time.
- Foundation for all other skill sets.
- Seeing the big picture—including daily tasks and the larger weekly and monthly schedule.
- Healthy sleep, eating, and exercise routines.
- Character strengths: grit and self-control.

PRIORITIZE
- Knowing what to tackle first, second, and third.
- Planning for long-term or multistep assignments.
- Solving problems in academic and social settings.
- Seeing the big picture—identifying main ideas and supporting details.
- Character strengths: optimism, curiosity, and social intelligence.

TAKE ACTION!
- Opposite of procrastination.
- Includes external motivation and internal motivation.
- Focus—or sustained attention—to the task at hand.
- Mindfulness skills help young learners get started on tasks.
- Character strengths: grit, optimism, self-control, curiosity, and zest.

REFLECT
- Self-awareness and metacognition.
- Flexibility—willingness to try a different approach.
- Connecting new knowledge to background knowledge.
- Mindfulness skills help young learners reflect.
- Character strengths: optimism, curiosity, gratitude, and social intelligence.

BALANCE
- Emotional regulation: identifying and coping with strong emotions.
- Emotional modulation: expressing feelings at an appropriate volume and time, especially when strong emotions arise.
- Impulse control and stress management.
- Effective communication and conflict resolution.
- Mindfulness skills support emotional balance.
- Character strengths: grit, self-control and social intelligence.

© 2017 Christina Young, *Executive Functions at Home and School*. Permission to photocopy this form is granted to purchasers of this book for personal and professional learning use only (see copyright page for details).

2 WHAT YOU NEED TO KNOW ABOUT MINDFULNESS, CHARACTER STRENGTHS, AND A GROWTH MINDSET

We view executive functions, mindfulness, and character strengths as three legs of a stool: Each is necessary to support a grounded, secure young learner. Add a growth mindset to this foundation, and watch the children in your life soar!

MINDFULNESS AND EXECUTIVE FUNCTIONS

One way to define mindfulness is the ability to pay attention in the moment and identify one's thoughts and feelings. That doesn't mean shutting off challenging feelings or imposing a facade of calm over feelings. It means acknowledging feelings without immediately reacting to them. For young learners, the practical skill of mindfulness is the ability to pause for a moment when experiencing a strong emotion in order to:

1. Take care of yourself by identifying the emotion and using a coping skill like deep breathing to balance the emotion.
2. Choose the best way to respond in this situation, using executive function skills or other skills—such as conflict-resolution skills—that you have learned.
3. Identify next steps, such as speaking to a parent or teacher, talking with a friend, or setting aside time that evening to work on a project.

Mindfulness skills are a necessary foundation for executive function skills. When young learners experience stressful situations or strong emotions, they will often *react* based on those emotions. To apply executive function skills, they need to first balance the emotional reaction in order to be able to *choose* how to best respond. For example, heightened stress at school because of an assignment or test can make it challenging for a student to access what they have learned about the material. In social settings, reacting immediately to strong emotions can increase conflict or result in unhealthy social decisions.

Additionally, young learners experience incredible physical, cognitive, and emotional growth and change through adolescence. Many young learners experience a sense of turmoil and insecurity during these changes, and their behavior is often a reaction to those uncomfortable emotions. Mindfulness skills help young learners identify and cope with emotions. In doing so, these learners gain self-awareness and self-confidence.

Mindfulness skills can be practiced using a variety of mindfulness exercises, including breathing exercises, guided relaxation, guided imagery, yoga, and meditation. Exercises such as walking, jogging, or swimming can become mindfulness practices by focusing on one's breath and one's body in the moment—for example, noticing the stream of thoughts in your mind and then consciously returning your focus to your breathing and your body's alignment as you move or noticing where there is tension that can be relaxed, such as a clenched jaw, and consciously relaxing it while exhaling. Deep breaths are often used in mindfulness practice, and it is a central mindfulness tool. Herbert Benson, M.D., documented the power of deep breathing exercises to counter the body's stress response in *The Relaxation Response*, published in 1975.[5]

Regular mindfulness practice can increase self-awareness and self-care. Young learners can use these mindfulness skills to respond to daily academic and personal challenges as well as larger unforeseen stressors that may arise. In response to an embarrassing situation at school, young learners with mindfulness skills may notice that their face feels hot and their stomach is in knots. Using a few deep breaths to "cool down" and relax the stomach puts them in a much better position to choose a response or move forward with the day.

Even short mindfulness exercises—such as those included in Chapters 7 and 8—can help manage stress and modulate emotional responses to stressors. When young learners are able to access their executive function or problem-solving skills and choose how to respond to an academic or social challenge, they gain self-confidence, self-awareness and reflection skills—all strong internal motivators.

Catch Your Breath

VIGNETTE

Ben headed for the kitchen and opened his mouth to yell for his mom. His brother was always doing this! Suddenly, Ben stopped. His brother was always doing this—if he called his mom right now, they would all end up having the exact same fight they had last night. Ben thought of his science teacher, Mr. Hoffman. When the class had a hard time getting to work, Mr. Hoffman would say, "OK, class. Let's take a minute to catch our breath." Ben went into his room and sat down on his bed. Next, Mr. Hoffman would ask the students to sit up straight and close their eyes, so Ben did that too. Then Mr. Hoffman would ask them to count out five deep breaths, in and out, along with him. Ben tried, but his first few breaths felt phony. In, out. One. In, out. Two. But then something changed. Ben felt his body relax a little, and the next breath felt like a real deep breath. Ben finished counting out five full breaths and opened his eyes. He was still mad at his brother, but he was also calmer. He thought about what he wanted his mom to know and how he wanted his mom to help. Then he headed for the kitchen again. "Hey, Mom," he said. "Can I talk to you?"

AN ABRIDGED HISTORY OF MINDFULNESS

Mindfulness, as widely understood in contemporary culture, originates from the work of psychologist Jon Kabat-Zinn. In 1979, Kabat-Zinn founded the Stress Reduction Clinic at the University of Massachusetts Medical School. He adapted Buddhist teachings on meditation and mindfulness through the lens of modern science to create a secular program that has evolved into today's Mindfulness-Based Stress Reduction (MBSR). Initially, medical professionals used mindfulness to help patients living with chronic pain. Long-term studies have documented its success.[6]

In the late 1980s, mental health professionals began using mindfulness to help patients living with a wide range of mental health disorders. Mindfulness is a core component of dialectical behavior therapy (DBT), which was originally used to treat patients with borderline personality disorder but is now used for a wide range of mental health disorders. By the 1990s, many mental health professionals were using Mindfulness-Based Cognitive Therapy (MBCT) to treat severe depression, attention deficits, and negative self-talk and to prevent substance-abuse relapse. Like MBSR, long-term studies have also documented DBT's success.[7]

Over the past 20 years, more and more educators have begun incorporating mindfulness into educational settings as a tool to help students get the most out of their time in the classroom. Ellen Langer is a social psychologist at Harvard University who has written extensively about mindfulness and learning.[8] Teaching mindfulness exercises at school is gaining increasing support from both administrators and classroom teachers. Research studies have shown that teaching mindfulness skills to students boosts impulse control and improves attention—two important components of a learning environment.[9] Researchers have begun to look at individual studies of mindfulness programs in schools in a larger context. Notably, positive effects are seen in cognitive performance, stress management, coping, and resilience.[10]

CHARACTER STRENGTHS AND EXECUTIVE FUNCTIONS

In our work with young learners, we observed that character strengths and executive function skills affect academic performance—intelligence and knowledge is just the starting point. Core character strengths and executive function skills determine how effectively you can build on that knowledge, how much you can achieve, and how well you balance achievement and wellbeing. Character strengths are personal qualities that can be supported and developed through conscious actions. Executive functions are skills that can be learned and strengthened through practice.

The Character Lab[11] is a nonprofit that focuses on character strengths. Its mission is to support research-based approaches to character that enable young learners to learn and flourish. The Character Lab defines character as "a person's disposition to think, feel, and act in ways that help oneself and others."[12] The Character Lab draws on the work of psychologist Martin Seligman, a central figure in the field of positive psychology, and specifically the 24 character strengths that Seligman identified as the core of positive psychology.[13] It builds on the work of Riverdale Country School and KIPP public charter schools in New York City. The two schools collaborated with Angela Duckworth, a MacArthur Fellow and Christopher H. Browne Distinguished Professor of Psychology at the University of Pennsylvania; Christopher Peterson, the former Arthur F. Thurnau Professor of Psychology and chair of clinical psychology at the University of Michigan and current science director of the VIA Institute on Character; and Seligman himself to identify seven key character strengths for young learners and create the specific indicators found in this chapter.

We find that the strengths highlighted by the Character Lab overlap with our key executive function skill sets, and we summarize that overlap here. We believe that teaching young learners to use and strengthen executive function skills also helps them develop more robust character strengths and vice versa.

TAKE NOTE

CHARACTER STRENGTHS

1. GRIT

- Finishes what they begin.
- Tries hard, even after experiencing failure.
- Works diligently and independently.

We believe that effective grit requires organization, prioritization, activation, reflection, and emotional balance skills. Encouraging young learners to "try harder" when they don't have these foundational skills can backfire. Young learners may be incredibly gritty in incredibly ineffective ways—with rigid or concrete thinking (often seen as stubbornness or defensiveness) and lacking cognitive flexibility—and then they are disappointed when their efforts do not pay off. Effective grit requires young learners to be self-aware and flexible. Supportive and constructive feedback is key to helping young learners cultivate grit. When faced with challenging tasks, young learners must implement effective strategies and value the necessary struggle involved in learning. Effective grit is at the core of the executive function skill of goal-directed persistence.[14]

2. OPTIMISM

- Sees failures and setbacks as temporary.
- Believes that effort will improve their future.
- Refuses to allow setbacks in one area to affect motivation in other areas.

TAKE NOTE

We think that optimism requires the skill of reflection and the flexibility to approach tasks in different ways. Productive optimism supports reflection on the causes of setbacks and problem solving. It is different from blind optimism, which may actually represent denial or inflexible thinking. In our experience, productive optimism helps young learners balance strong emotions.

3. SELF-CONTROL—SCHOOLWORK

- Comes to class prepared.
- Pays attention and resists distractions.
- Remembers and follows directions.
- Gets to work right away, rather than procrastinating.

We consider planning to be a core component of this character strength. Planning prior to working supports effective effort, and realistic plans support productive optimism and help young learners take action. In our experience, self-control—schoolwork requires the executive function skills of organization, prioritization, activation, reflection and emotional balance. Mindfulness skills support this character strength.

SELF-CONTROL—INTERPERSONAL

- Remains calm even when criticized or otherwise provoked.
- Allows others to speak without interruption.
- Is polite to adults and peers.
- Keeps temper in check.

In our experience, self-control—interpersonal requires the executive function skills of prioritization, reflection and emotional balance. Mindfulness skills support this character strength.

4. CURIOSITY

- Pursues opportunities for independent learning.
- Is eager to explore new things.
- Asks and answers questions to deepen their understanding.

We observe that curiosity fuels the executive function skills of prioritization, activation, and reflection, and vice versa.

5. ZEST

- Shows enthusiasm.
- Invigorates others with their energy.
- Actively participates.

We believe that activation supports zest and zest supports activation. Zest illustrates a little discussed side of emotional balance, allowing positive emotions to motivate oneself as well as others.

6. GRATITUDE

- Reciprocates kindness from peers and teachers.
- Recognizes and shows appreciation for others.
- Recognizes and shows appreciation for their opportunities.

We believe that gratitude both requires and boosts reflection and balance. Gratitude supports activation by increasing internal motivation and optimism. Mindfulness skills cultivate gratitude.

7. SOCIAL INTELLIGENCE

- Able to find solutions during conflicts with others.
- Demonstrates respect for others' feelings.
- Knows when and how to include others.
- Adapts effectively in different situations.

We view a large component of social intelligence as the ability to see the big picture through organization, prioritization, reflection, emotional balance and mindfulness.

We agree with the Character Lab's belief that character is as important as academics in leading a meaningful, successful life. We view character strengths and mindfulness as two elements of emotional intelligence, which comprises five domains:[15]

1. Knowing your emotions.
2. Managing your emotions.
3. Motivating yourself.
4. Recognizing and understanding other people's emotions.
5. Managing relationships.

These five domains are reflected in the key executive function skill sets, our definition of mindfulness and mindfulness skills, and the Character Lab's seven key character strengths. We believe that to effectively apply academic knowledge and work to their full potential, young learners must develop emotional intelligence—and that includes executive functions, mindfulness, and character strengths.

In our work, we often connect executive function skills to character strengths. The following chart illustrates the connections we have worked to cultivate in young learners.

TAKE NOTE

OVERLAP OF CHARACTER STRENGTHS AND EXECUTIVE FUNCTIONS

GRIT	<ul><li>Finishes whatever he or she begins.</li><li>Tries hard even after failure.</li><li>Works diligently and independently.</li></ul>	**Organize Prioritize Take Action! Reflect Balance**
OPTIMISM	<ul><li>Sees failures and setbacks as temporary.</li><li>Believes that effort will improve his or her future.</li><li>Refuses to allow setbacks in one area to affect motivation in other areas.</li></ul>	**Reflect Take Action! Balance**
SELF-CONTROL—SCHOOLWORK	<ul><li>Comes to class prepared and gets to work.</li><li>Pays attention and resists distractions.</li><li>Remembers and follows directions.</li></ul>	**Organize Prioritize Take Action! Balance**
SELF-CONTROL—INTERPERSONAL	<ul><li>Remains calm, even when criticized or otherwise provoked.</li><li>Allows others to speak without interruption and is polite to adults and peers.</li></ul>	**Prioritize Reflect Balance**
CURIOSITY	<ul><li>Pursues opportunities for independent learning.</li><li>Is eager to explore new things.</li><li>Asks and answers questions to deepen understanding.</li></ul>	**Prioritize Take Action! Reflect**
ZEST	<ul><li>Shows enthusiasm.</li><li>Invigorates others with his or her energy.</li><li>Actively participates.</li></ul>	**Take Action! Balance**
GRATITUDE	<ul><li>Reciprocates kindness.</li><li>Recognizes and shows appreciation.</li><li>Recognizes and appreciates opportunities.</li></ul>	**Take Action! Reflect Balance**
SOCIAL INTELLIGENCE	<ul><li>Finds solutions during conflicts.</li><li>Respects others' feelings.</li><li>Knows when and how to include others.</li><li>Adapts effectively in different situations.</li></ul>	**Organize Prioritize Reflect Balance**

© 2017 Christina Young, *Executive Functions at Home and School*. Character strengths and indicators used with permission from the Character Lab. Permission to photocopy this form is granted to purchasers of this book for personal and professional learning use only (see copyright page for details).

GROWTH MINDSET AND EXECUTIVE FUNCTIONS

In our work with young learners, we see that a student's mindset can have a huge impact on his or her academic growth. There are two basic mindsets: a growth mindset and a fixed mindset. The definitions below are based on the work of psychologist and researcher Carol Dweck.[16]

Students with a **fixed mindset** believe their intelligence or talent is a fixed trait. For example, some young learners base their identity on being "smart," and they focus on proving how intelligent they are instead of challenging themselves to grow. Others may try hard in class and complete homework, but they still attribute their own or others' performance to a predetermined ability or talent. Dweck's research indicates that these students often resist taking on academic challenges. They may dismiss entire topics as something "I'm not good at."

We often observe that students who seem to have a fixed mindset mistakenly believe they should be able to hold most information in their head, rather than use organizational tools. They do not realize that using a planning system or an outline for a writing assignment can free up working memory or "head space" to use on high-level or critical-thinking tasks. (Chapter 4 discusses working memory in depth.) As a result, they can experience a lot of frustration when the work they produce does not appear to represent their abilities. Students with a fixed mindset also seem less inclined to reflect on their academic work and less flexible regarding alternative approaches to assignments. Perhaps because they mistakenly believe that "smart" students shouldn't have to work hard.

Students with a **growth mindset** believe their abilities can be developed through hard work and practice. They understand that learning requires challenge and that it can feel uncomfortable and difficult as you work toward that aha! moment of understanding. When students understand how to work effectively and use active study strategies to practice skills in a deliberate way, a growth mindset can support grit, curiosity, and zest. When teaching students about a growth mindset, it's critical that you help them identify effective work habits. The following section on the foundations of active learning, the discussions following each vignette in Chapter 5, and the strategies in Chapters 7 and 8 all support effective and active work.

"Working hard" in ineffective ways—such as putting a lot of effort into an assignment without understanding and following the instructions—can backfire and lead to frustration and decreased motivation, unwittingly encouraging a fixed mindset in young learners. Additionally, a young learner who struggles with perfectionism may misinterpret growth mindset in a way that validates a tendency to overwork in ineffective ways and makes it even harder to modulate their effort. Although a growth mindset can be a powerful and positive attribute, it is nuanced. As with so many other aspects of learning, young learners need specific, supportive feedback from adults.

Dweck herself has written about the importance of recognizing and overcoming a false growth mindset.[17] She identifies four major challenges to supporting a true growth mindset.

TAKE NOTE

1. **Praising Effort Alone:** It is important to acknowledge the work *process*—the effort and strategies employed on a task. But praising ineffective effort—work that does not support learning, comprehension, and a stronger product—can backfire and become a consolation prize that dismisses young learners who are not "smart." When students are not successful, saying "good try" isn't helpful. It is important to support them in identifying what went wrong and implementing more effective strategies.

2. **Telling Young Learners "You Can Do Anything":** It is important to set the bar high for young learners—and then teach them the strategies and tools that can help them reach those goals. But when students don't yet have the knowledge or skills to succeed at a task, this kind of blanket statement can easily backfire and reinforce a fixed mindset.

3. **Blaming the Young Learner's Mindset:** Reprimanding or judging young learners because you think they have a "fixed mindset" can be shaming and detrimental to the very skills you are trying to teach. It requires courage and resilience for young learners to take a growth mindset approach to tackling new and challenging tasks. To develop a growth mindset approach, students need honest and supportive feedback, recommended learning strategies, and opportunities to revise their work and see improvement.

4. **Overcoming Perceived Threats:** A fixed mindset can be triggered by something that a young learner perceives as threatening—perhaps a fear of mistakes or failure. It's natural to lean toward a fixed mindset in some areas and a growth mindset in others. Reflecting on your own journey as a parent or teacher through the fixed mindset and growth mindset approaches you take in different areas can provide valuable insight into the experiences of the young learners in your life. Simply put, it's easier to embrace a growth mindset approach when you feel confident, and it's easy to fall into a fixed mindset approach when you're out of your comfort zone.

Of course, a lot of deep, enduring learning happens outside of our comfort zone. Mindfulness and emotional balance skills help young learners cope with the necessary discomfort inherent in learning and cultivate a growth mindset approach. Other key executive function skill sets build confidence and a sense of independence that helps young learners see the connections among their efforts, their growth, and their accomplishments.

Taking these nuances into account, parents and teachers can support a growth mindset approach to learning by using language that values the young learner's process of applying effective effort and using strategies and tools to gain knowledge, strengthen comprehension, and learn actively. When a young learner is successful, praise their efforts or the work they put in, rather than just the product, grade, or what you judge to be their innate intelligence.

For example:

> "You worked on organizing and revising your writing, and your final essay is stronger because of it."

> "You made a thoughtful study plan for this test, and I saw a lot of improvement."

> "That assignment had a lot of steps. I see that you stuck with it and responded to every part."

When young learners feel unsuccessful, your response can help them face the challenge with a growth mindset approach:

> "Feeling frustrated and unsure is part of learning something new. I can see that you care a lot about this class."

> "This unit is harder for you. Let's keep working on ways to help you understand the material. You will get the hang of it."

> Student: "I'm just not good at math!"
> Teacher: "You don't feel confident doing algebra *yet*! You need more help right now and then more practice."

Young learners are always watching us, even when we think they're not listening. Be aware of the way you talk about others. If you have a habit of casually labeling a person based on what you judge to be personal attributes, your children or students may do the same to themselves.

The most common fixed mindset reinforcer is "smart." Often used as a compliment—"You're so smart" or "She's so smart"—it feeds young learners' tendency to constantly rank themselves on a hierarchy of smart.

Here are other examples of fixed mindset reinforcers:

"He's not the brightest bulb."

"She's always been great at school."

"He's a natural."

"She'll never be a rocket scientist."

At its best, a growth mindset builds motivation and self-esteem *and* leads to higher levels of academic achievement. Students with a growth mindset approach to learning embrace academic challenges, and they use organizational tools and study strategies to produce their best work. They are not afraid to tackle a tough subject, even when it doesn't go well at first, and they are open to learning from mistakes. They are comfortable seeking help and collaborating with others—be it a teacher, parent, or peer. They are courageous and resilient learners.

THE FOUNDATIONS OF ACTIVE LEARNING

Effective learning is *effortful*. Although spending a lot of time "studying" does not equal effective learning, effective learning does require both time and effort. By effective learning, we mean learning that endures and can be applied to both current and future tasks. The book *Make It Stick*[18] illustrates how common study strategies such as rereading and reviewing—and cramming before a test—fail to lead to deeper, long-term understanding and mastery. More active and more effortful strategies may seem harder and more slowgoing in the moment, but they lead to greater understanding and long-term success.

Make It Stick provides detailed descriptions and examples of three study strategies that comprise the foundation of active and durable learning: spaced practice, retrieval practice, and interleaving. A growth mindset approach to learning supports these strategies, and these strategies support a

growth mindset. Executive function skills are required to consistently and effectively use these strategies. Chapter 8 includes active study strategies that build on these three foundational strategies.

Spaced practice is spacing out your active practice at a task. It is the opposite of massing practice—or cramming—in order to memorize information before a test. Using spaced practice, young learners engage in a consistent study plan—through active study strategies—in shorter work sessions spread over time. An example is applying more effort on nightly math homework and creating a study schedule a week before the unit test to identify and practice challenging problems for an extra 20 minutes each night.

Practicing in shorter sessions spaced out over time—and then taking a break to work on other subjects, participate in other activities, and get a good night's sleep—means the young learner will need to actively re-engage in the subject at the start of each study session. Re-engaging with the material after a break supports developing a deeper understanding of those facts and concepts. Massed practice—or cramming—results in more surface recall of information crammed into fewer, longer sessions. Cramming "works" as a way to remember information for the short term. It does not work as a way to learn deeply, retain information, and apply that information to future tasks.[19]

Retrieval practice is retrieving—or recalling—information from memory. Instead of rereading text or reviewing notes, young learners challenge themselves to retrieve information from their long-term memory. The ubiquitous student favorite—flashcards and the computerized version popularized by Quizlet—is an example of retrieval practice. Flashcards are an effective way to learn rote facts such as Spanish vocabulary, but the next step in retrieval practice is putting those facts into context by creating sentences or having a conversation in Spanish. Taking practice tests or low-stakes quizzes are also examples of retrieval practice. Retrieval practice is more active and effective than the passive study strategies of rereading and reviewing.

Interleaving is intentionally rotating between practice for different tasks or subjects. For example, making a homework or study plan to work on history for 30 minutes and then switching to Spanish vocabulary for 30 minutes, taking a short break, going back to study history for 30 minutes, and ending with 30 minutes of Spanish.

When young learners shift their focus between subjects—just like in spaced practice—they must frequently re-engage with the material. In the short term, retrieving or recalling the facts and concepts for each subject may feel "harder" or more effortful. It may even feel less productive in the short term. But the effort expended in interleaving learning between subjects supports stronger recall and understanding of those subjects. It produces deeper learning that will endure over time. In other words, students will remember what they learn when it's spread out over time and understand subjects much better than when they cram before a high-stakes test.

Many active study strategies get a boost in effectiveness when young learners practice **elaborative interrogation**.[20] Simply put, prompting students to answer "Why" questions leads to deeper, more durable learning. So elaborative interrogation is a method of asking and answering questions based on the text that pushes young learners to answer not just "What," but also "Why," "How," and

TAKE NOTE

"Where does it connect" to previous or upcoming information. As a bonus, practicing elaborative interrogation inherently builds the skill of academic reflection.

THE MYTH OF MULTITASKING

It is important to distinguish interleaving from multitasking. Interleaving is working solely on one task or subject for a period of time—often 30 minutes or more—before consciously wrapping up that work session, transitioning to another task or subject, and then coming back to the first task after a longer period of time.

Multitasking is often misunderstood to mean doing two or more things at the same time. In reality, multitasking is switching quickly between two or more tasks. For any reasonably complex mental task, it is impossible to multitask effectively, unless one of the tasks has become virtually automatic through extensive practice.

How does multitasking affect performance? The brain makes two separate decisions before a task switch: It determines a new task goal, and it identifies a new set of rules for the task.[21] In contrast, interleaving approaches this transition in an intentional, sequential, and focused way. Here's an example of how this switching looks when a student "multitasks."

> Jeremy is doing history homework with his smartphone next to his laptop. A new text arrives, and he pauses his homework to read and answer it. This is a new goal.
> - Jeremy's brain "turns off" the goal and rules of the history task: identifying key factors of the French Revolution.
> - It "turns on" reading and responding to the smartphone text. This requires a new goal of answering the text and a different set of rules: Who is the text from? What social norms determine the type of response?

This switch happens *every time* Jeremy "multitasks" his homework and his texts. The process of determining the new goal and rules for the next task can happen in less than a second, but it still takes time. The more Jeremy switches between these tasks—homework and texting—the more time is devoted to new goals and rules.

This is the hidden cost of multitasking: It often takes much longer to complete two tasks through multitasking than it would take to complete the same tasks sequentially in a more intentional way. There are additional, significant costs of multitasking—especially as more back-and-forth switching occurs: Performance quality often declines *and* processing becomes less deep for each task. This usually means that less enduring memories are encoded and learning suffers. (See Chapter 4 for more information on memory and learning.) These costs are amplified when the tasks involved are more cognitively complex.

Perhaps the biggest challenge with multitasking is that the person switching back and forth between tasks quickly and without focused intention often has very little, awareness that by doing it, they are spending more time, performing less well and learning less.[22] As Jeremy continues texting, his effort applied to history is becoming less and less effective, even though he will spend more time on his homework due to all the texting interruptions. His work time will be far more effective if he silences his phone, focuses on history for 30 minutes, and then takes a five-minute break to respond to texts.

WHAT'S THE BIG PICTURE?

Executive function skills are required for academic and personal achievement, but they alone cannot support young learners in reaching their potential. Mindfulness and character strengths—both components of emotional intelligence—determine how effectively young learners can apply their knowledge to academic and personal challenges. Additionally, a true growth mindset helps young learners understand that while working and learning effectively may take more effort and feel less comfortable at first, it will pay off in the long run. Mindfulness, character strengths, and a growth mindset each support active learning. Active learning requires more effort up front, but it leads to deeper, more durable learning.

NOW WHAT?

- Incorporate short mindfulness exercises into your work with young learners. We include resources in Chapters 7 and 8.
- Teach young learners about character strengths and actions that build those strengths. Refer to these actions in your ongoing work together.
- Talk with young learners about the immediate and long-term benefits of the active study approaches of spaced practice, retrieval practice, and interleaving.

What is an area in which you tend to have fixed mindset? What is an area in which you tend to have a growth mindset?

Think of a few young learners in your life. What stood out to you in this chapter as especially relevant to supporting them?

WHAT MAKES ALL OF THIS SO IMPORTANT?

A STRENGTHS AND SKILLS APPROACH

For many academic and behavioral challenges, using a strengths-based approach allows you to take a step back and identify the young learner's specific strengths and challenges—or skills and skill deficits—without triggering defensiveness. This approach helps parents and teachers in three major ways.

1. IT EMPOWERS AND MOTIVATES YOUNG LEARNERS

When working with a young learner, ask them to identify strengths: What's going well? What are they feeling good about? What was effective about the effort they put into an assignment or event? Encourage them to look beyond academics and grades: Are they involved in a co-curricular activity or a sport? Have they had a recent positive experience outside of school? Acknowledging young learners' strengths and including their own voice in the assessment of their strengths and challenges will help create an emotionally safe environment, where they feel seen and validated as a whole person, rather than judged as a "bad student" or "stupid." When young learners feel emotionally safe, they have more access to the prefrontal cortex and key executive function skills.

One way of beginning this dialogue is through metaphor, which can be a powerful teaching tool. For example, a student who is a confident athlete but struggles with a fixed mindset toward schoolwork may easily relate to sports metaphors that support a growth mindset approach to schoolwork. By taking a wider view of your student or child, you can help them access more of their own resources.

2. IT IDENTIFIES AND IMPLEMENTS TARGETED SUPPORT

Once you've identified strengths, look at academic or behavioral challenges. Partnering with the young learner, identify the specific skill deficit or ineffective work habit that is causing the most problems. (Chapter 6 discusses using a coach approach to partner with young learners.) Consider the young learner's social, emotional, and physical health. Perhaps before focusing on academic goals, making changes to sleep habits, nutrition, or exercise would be beneficial. Be selective—choose one or two skills to work on at first, and use small, realistic short-term goals to support sustainable change. (Chapter 5 includes more information on setting realistic short-term goals.)

Once you've identified a specific skill deficit, choose a tool or strategy to bolster that skill. It may be a concrete tool, like a monthly calendar or a paragraph organizer. It may be reading-based discussions intended to develop more abstract skills, like identifying main ideas and supporting details. There are times when practicing mindfulness exercises or teaching about such character strengths as grit or curiosity can make a big difference. For young learners in the grip of a fixed mindset, discussing how to cultivate a growth mindset approach to work can be empowering.

3. IT SUPPORTS PARENTS AND TEACHERS

When an adolescent in whom you are deeply invested struggles, you can feel anywhere from frustrated to heartbroken. It can wreak havoc on your family's home life or the learning environment in your classroom. Taking a skills and strengths view can support your own emotional regulation and modulation. When challenges persist over time, parents and teachers can fall into challenging patterns, such as nagging, scolding, avoiding the issue until it blows up or—perhaps the most challenging—the cycle of blame. We've seen plenty of students fall into this cycle too.

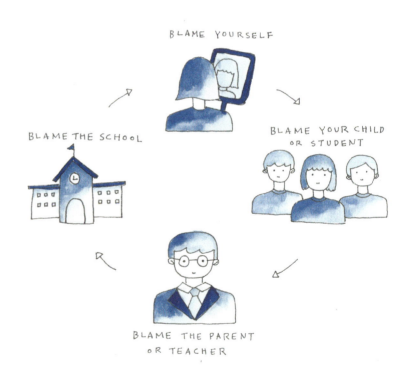

Reviewing a young learner's executive function skills, mindfulness skills, character strengths, and mindset can provide a welcome perspective that allows you to separate your emotional response from the current challenges. It can help you find patience and a fresh approach.

ADHD AND OTHER LEARNING DIFFERENCES

The executive function challenges that all young learners experience are often exacerbated for those diagnosed with ADHD or other learning differences.

Many, but not all, ADHD symptoms are connected to significant challenges with working memory or executive functions. (Chapter 4 covers information on memory, including working memory.) We often observe that teens with ADHD take in a higher level of information or stimulation from their environment. They can easily become overloaded by the information they take in throughout the day, in part because they do not have the ability or skills to filter—or prioritize—the information effectively. They could have difficulty organizing information before storing it in their memory or after it's retrieved from memory. Developing stronger executive function skills is often an important part of a comprehensive treatment plan for ADHD.

TAKE NOTE

PSYCHOEDUCATIONAL EVALUATION

Ongoing challenges with executive functions may indicate an underlying learning difference.

Parents: If you are concerned that the challenges you observe are connected to a greater underlying challenge, a comprehensive psychoeducational evaluation administered by a licensed psychologist—also referred to as a neuropsychological evaluation—can help you identify underlying causes and plan effective interventions. A comprehensive evaluation includes tests designed to measure skills and abilities in several domains, including cognitive functioning, memory, processing speed, visual–spatial skills, auditory skills, reading comprehension, math skills, attention, executive function skills, and psychosocial skills. An evaluation can diagnose language-based, math-based, and nonverbal learning disabilities. It can also uncover working memory challenges, processing speed challenges, executive function challenges, or other cognitive challenges that may not meet the criteria for a diagnosis

TAKE NOTE

but still provide relevant information to help you better support your child academically and personally.

A psychoeducational evaluation may also include a test to assess a child's intelligent quotient or IQ. Even adolescents with average to high IQs can face enormous challenges personally and academically if they are not able to develop strong executive function skills. IQ is a score determined by one's performance on a standardized intelligence test relative to the average performance of others of the same age. IQ is considered to be a universal, standardized indicator of intellectual ability. Executive functions, however, impact how well an individual is able to use that ability.

A young learner with a high IQ and poor executive function skills will have a difficult time expressing ideas clearly and may experience a high level of frustration that affects behavior and relationships with parents, teachers, and peers.

If school administrators or personal treatment providers recommend an evaluation, it is likely because they believe that it will provide valuable information on observed challenges and potential interventions. For example, a school may recommend an evaluation due to a pattern of observed academic or behavioral challenges across several courses in one year or in a specific course across several years. At its best, an evaluation report is like a road map to your child's learning process, including strengths, challenges, and recommended interventions for home and school. The insight and information an evaluation process provides can be incredibly helpful and empowering for a young learner who has been struggling without understanding the factors that are negatively influencing experiences and accomplishments at home and school.

In our experience, the most informative and beneficial evaluation reports do more than document the data from testing and, if applicable, diagnoses. They include:

- Relevant context—family history, previous evaluations and challenges, previous interventions, concerns noted by parents, and teachers and parent observations.

- Comprehensive reports from school—including grades and teacher observations of academic performance, classroom behavior, and social skills.
- An analysis of the results that illustrate the real-world impact on the child's learning.
- A professional narrative that supports the interventions recommended by the evaluator.
- Specific recommendations for real-world support or interventions, both in *and* outside of school.

The American Psychological Association provides information and guidelines for evaluations.[23] Speak to your school's student support services with questions or concerns about how the school will respond to the report and consider its recommendations. At most schools, evaluation reports are treated with respect and confidentiality, and they are not documented on report cards or disclosed by the school when a student applies to secondary schools or colleges. School policy varies regarding how much information is disclosed to teachers. It's beneficial to understand your school's evaluation and accommodation policies before starting the process.

WHAT'S THE BIG PICTURE?

Looking at challenges through the lenses of executive functions, mindfulness, character strengths, and a growth mindset can help parents and teachers take a strengths-based approach to their work with young learners.

Identifying strengths and skills—academic, athletic, artistic, or social—frames your work together positively. Identifying specific challenges or skill deficits helps set productive goals and target support.

Using these lenses also helps parents and teachers regulate and modulate their own emotional responses to the struggles they witness. When these struggles persist across disciplines or over time, it may be time to consider a psychoeducational evaluation to determine if there is an underlying learning difference.

NOW WHAT?

Think of one young learner in your life. What do you see as their strengths?

Are you concerned there may be an underlying challenge? Describe it here.

- Ask the young learner to describe their strengths. Do they identify the same strengths that you did?
- If you have concerns about underlying challenges, speak to your child's treatment provider or student support services at school.

WHAT'S IMPORTANT TO KNOW ABOUT MEMORY AND ATTENTION?

Working memory and attention impact most executive function skills. They also play a critical role in learning. This chapter reviews some of the key components of memory and attention.

MEMORY

There is a wealth of recent research on memory and learning.[24] This chapter provides relevant context in broad strokes.

Memory is the ability to receive, process, store, and retrieve information. The main categories for memory are sensory memory, short-term memory—including working memory—and long-term memory.

Sensory memory takes in information from the five senses. When the sensory stimuli ceases, that information is either transferred to short-term memory or discarded.

Short-term memory consists of briefly registering new information and determining if it is needed immediately, useful for a future task, or unnecessary. An example is temporarily remembering a short string of numbers. Information that is needed immediately or useful for a future task may be transferred to long-term memory if some effort is applied to learn the information. Information that is briefly registered but considered unnecessary is discarded—or forgotten.

Working memory mentally suspends selected information while using or manipulating it. We often describe working memory as the surface area of a small desk. It is the workplace for things you are currently processing. If a young learner goes through the school day piling more and more papers on that desk without organizing or prioritizing the information, it's going to become increasingly difficult to pull out the paper they need for class. More and more papers will pile up and shift around until they fall off the desk at random. This is how young learners can forget things you can't believe they've forgotten—they overload their working memory. We often see students who clutter their working memory with assignments and details they think they can "remember," instead of recording them in a planner or calendar. In fact, they are limiting the working space available for critical thinking—understanding concepts or synthesizing information to build an academic argument.

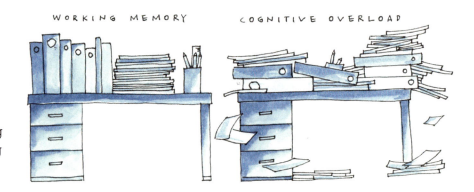

Overloading working memory is also referred to as **cognitive overload.** Executive function skills can alleviate cognitive overload. Greater underlying challenges with working memory are assessed as part of a comprehensive psychoeducational evaluation.

Here are two examples of how working memory challenges may show up at school. Both students experience significant executive function skill deficits that are related to underlying working memory challenges. (Chapter 5 includes more examples of executive function challenges, along with strategies to support the young learner.)

> Alex is having a hard time in eighth grade. He is withdrawn and irritated most of the time at school. He believes that he understands the material, and he gets frustrated when his English and history teachers ask him to show his work on outlines or rewrite paragraph assignments. In math class, he has trouble solving multistep problems. When he meets with his teachers, Alex seems to understand the major concepts, yet when he has to articulate his understanding in an assignment that includes a few different tasks, his responses are often off-track. Alex seems disorganized, and he leaves his coat or backpack behind in class a few times each day.

> Julianne is a ninth-grade student struggling to adjust to the demands of high school. In class, she will often raise her hand and then forget what she wants to say. She feels overwhelmed by the material covered in her classes, and she has a hard time listening while taking notes. Julianne finds the reading in English and history much harder this year, and her grades have dropped significantly in those classes. Julianne's teachers observe several challenges in her writing: unorganized information that does not support her thesis statement, failure to address all the parts of the prompts or questions, and frequent spelling and grammar errors.

Long-term memory stores information after the learner has actively engaged with it. Active learning includes creating an association with prior or background knowledge, categorizing the information, recognizing patterns, and practicing skills. Long-term memory is both the broadest and most nuanced category of memory. It includes implicit memory—which allows one to do things by rote—and explicit memory—which requires conscious thought. What teachers often refer to as "automaticity" refers to the ability to do some things that are encoded in long-term memory by rote—or automatically.

Here are examples of the importance of automaticity.

- In language arts, proficiency or automaticity in basic grammar is required to express ideas clearly in writing assignments. An inability to craft simple and compound sentences clearly or correctly punctuate one's writing makes it difficult to communicate more sophisticated literary analyses in writing.

- A middle-school student who has not memorized and achieved automaticity in the basic multiplication tables will require more time to complete algebra problems. The need to spend more time on basic computation—and the increased likelihood of multiplication errors—will make every quiz and test more stressful and harder to complete in the allotted time.

Automaticity develops through repeated practice. A lack of automaticity is one reason for "careless errors." When more time and thinking is required to execute basic tasks, it is likely that the student will end up either losing focus or rushing. Young learners generally care a lot about their academic performance. These errors can more accurately be described as detail errors, copying errors, assumption errors, or rushing errors.

Memory and Learning

In the book *Why Don't Students Like School,*[25] cognitive scientist and psychologist Daniel Willingham describes memory as the residue of thought. In other words, you must think in order to learn. Consider a student creating a presentation through PowerPoint on the branches of government. If the student thinks mostly about creating

TAKE NOTE

the presentation while quickly copying in the content, then he or she will learn how to use the presentation program but will retain little about the branches of government.

Thinking is using one's mind to consider or reason about something. Often, young learners will stay on the surface of a task—focused on answering the basic question or solving the basic problem. Beginning in middle school, young learners are asked to think "abstractly." As Willingham describes, they are asked to think in terms of functions or deep structure. That includes connecting new information to previously learned material and grouping ideas into categories based on main ideas and supporting details. This allows students to elaborate—to make inferences and then describe or support them. Deep thinking is challenging, tiring, uncertain work, and it requires guidance and practice. To support young learners, it is useful to discuss the purpose of the assignment before they begin, so they are able to finish "I am learning this because…" and "This connects to the current topic because…"

Willingham also explores the value of stories as teaching tools, because we tend to remember what stirs emotions in us. We can use stories to teach concepts or use a story structure to plan a lesson. This connection between emotion and learning also speaks to the importance of building a strong rapport with the young learners in your lives.

Rapport refers to a relationship in which the individuals understand the nature of the relationship (for example, student-teacher), communicate well, recognize each other's feelings and ideas, and treat each other with consistent kindness and respect. When young learners are confident in that rapport, they feel emotionally safe—and therefore more open to dialogue and feedback.

Parents and teachers often experience the difference that having a strong rapport makes with young learners. Cognitive science[26] shows that learning happens most effectively when young learners sense the connection and support that makes them feel secure enough to engage actively with new information. This is sometimes referred to as "challenge with assurance."[27] When students feel assured of that rapport, they are more likely to:

- Raise their hand to answer a question in front of classmates.
- Look at an event from a different perspective (exhibiting cognitive flexibility).
- Acknowledge when they are confused or off-track, instead of disengaging from the lesson or distracting their peers.

ATTENTION

Working memory is an important underlying component to strong executive function skills. Another vital component is attention, or the ability to concentrate on a current source of information. "Paying attention" involves five specific skills:[28]

1. **Focusing on or attending to a single task**—being present and alert for class instructions or an interaction with a parent.

2. **Initiating or activating one's attention**—ending a casual conversation with a classmate in order to take out the materials needed for class and direct attention to the teacher without being prompted by an adult.

3. **Sustaining or maintaining concentration**—after being distracted in class by a joke or another interruption, returning focus to one's notes, the current activity, or the teacher.

4. **Inhibiting or blocking out external and internal distractions**—remaining focused on the teacher and not engaging with a peer who is distracting or disruptive. This includes noticing when one has been daydreaming and returning attention to the class activity.

5. **Changing focus as a task or class requires without becoming distracted or disengaging**—moving from a mini lesson to an activity without requiring repeated prompting from the teacher or engaging in chitchat with classmates.

To say that a student is not "paying attention" is a generalization that can cause a lot of frustration without helping to develop relevant skills. It is much more effective to identify which discrete skill the student is struggling with and offer strategies to strengthen it.

Students in middle and high school are expected to "pay attention" for eight hours a day with limited breaks for P.E. and lunch. Classes last an average 45 minutes, and many classes still use a lecture format. Most adolescents will experience short lapses in attention every few minutes—from the start of class and throughout the lesson.[29] This means that it's crucial for teachers to periodically pause and provide opportunities for young learners to engage actively with the information. For example:

- Pause instruction and ask students to sum up the main idea and supporting details.
- Highlight the concept, and ask students to relate it to previously covered concepts.
- Introduce a class activity or partner activity.

We recommend that teachers slow down their delivery of new content and provide plenty of cues to support student engagement and note taking. We find that giving students time to think *before* writing notes boosts their understanding of key concepts, as well as their performance on tests. (More note-taking strategies are included in Chapter 8.)

For parents, it is important to know that your child will have difficulty sustaining attention in a lengthy conversation. Repeating points or concepts in a longer conversation or giving lengthy examples does not help your child retain the information. Parents and teachers can apply interleaving, a tool discussed in Chapter 2, for productive dialogue with young learners. It is more useful to have a short dialogue that serves to either begin a series of dialogues on a topic or set a clear goal. Over time, continue the dialogue in short segments to reflect on recent topics, goals, and actions or introduce new ones. Listen as much, or more, than you talk. It may take some time to get used to this new rhythm of communication, but the payoff is a child who is more able and willing to engage in shorter, more frequent dialogue. Chapters 5 and 6 include more information on setting goals and engaging young learners in productive dialogue.

WHAT'S THE BIG PICTURE?

Previous chapters note that telling young learners to "work harder" without helping them to identify and implement effective, active study strategies can backfire and result in increased challenges and frustration. Likewise, judging that a young learner is "lazy" or "doesn't care" without considering possible challenges in working memory and attention can reinforce a negative self-view that makes it harder to try new strategies, engage in work, and cultivate a growth mindset. Understanding the key components of memory and attention provides another lens for understanding and supporting the challenges of the young learners in your life.

NOW WHAT?

Think of a few young learners in your life. What challenges may relate to overloading their working memory?

Review the five components of "paying attention." Which ones are the biggest challenges for them?

- Ask for feedback from school to see if teachers and staff have similar observations.
- Strategies to strengthen executive functions can also support working memory and attention.

HOW EXECUTIVE FUNCTION CHALLENGES LOOK AT HOME AND SCHOOL

This chapter looks more deeply at the six key executive function skill sets for young learners and the challenges they often face at home and school. After the description of each skill set is a vignette illustrating how a specific challenge may play out. Each vignette is followed by an assessment of the challenges depicted along with strategies to intervene. (Chapters 7 and 8 contain additional strategies and resources.)

Because these skill sets overlap and build on one another, it is important to consider how each skill set relates to the others.

1. ORGANIZE

This skill set includes three foundational components for strong executive functions:

1. **Time and material management**—the ability to put information and materials in a useful order. This includes identifying the steps and scheduling the time needed to complete a task.
2. **Sense of time**—an awareness of the passage of time, the ability to accurately estimate how long a task will take, and the ability to adjust plans and actions to meet time constraints or schedule changes.
3. **Nutrition, exercise, and sleep**—because each positively impacts execution function skills, thinking and learning, and overall wellbeing, we include them here in our foundational executive function skill set.[30] Chapter 7 includes more information on the impact of nutrition, exercise, and sleep.

Organization skills allow young learners to shift from using parents or teachers as their primary organizational tool to taking responsibility for their own work and schedule.

Organization skills are foundational skills required to succeed both personally and academically. They are the most concrete executive functions, so they are a great place to start. Organization tasks can be clearly defined, and young learners can often readily identify where they are lacking these skills. They develop the ability to see the big picture and plan accordingly. Healthy sleep, eating, and exercise routines support social, emotional, and physical wellbeing. For all these reasons, organization is a great place to begin implementing strategies to strengthen executive functions. This vignette illustrates one way that lack of time and material management can affect a young learner at home and at school.

VIGNETTE

Time and Material Management

Liam is in seventh grade. His grades are usually Bs or high Cs, and his teachers believe he is not working to his full potential. When he participates in class, he seems to understand the material and contributes in a meaningful way. But his participation is inconsistent, and some days he does not seem to be following class at all. His teachers are especially concerned about his lack of organization. His papers frequently fall out of his binders. He often fails to turn in homework assignments, and when he does, the paper is creased or crumpled. At home, discussions about the mess in Liam's room quickly escalate to yelling. His parents have tried taking away electronics and other privileges, but nothing motivates Liam to be more organized.

Liam's challenges with time and material management are negatively affecting his ability to engage in class and learn. At home, those challenges are a consistent cause of stress and tension that are taking a toll on the parent–child relationship. Liam's teachers and parents frequently ask him to "be more organized," but Liam does not understand what that means or how to do it. He is beginning to believe that he just isn't "good at school."

When asked what's different about his classes this year, Liam reports that each class starts and ends differently. In sixth grade, most of his teachers still had an agenda on the board at the start of class and prompted the students multiple times to take out their planners and hand in homework. This year, Liam's teachers expect the students to enter the classroom, turn in the homework, and get out what they need for class autonomously. The class begins more quickly, and the lesson usually goes right to the end of the period. The teachers tell the students to check a website for the homework. Liam has not adjusted to these new academic expectations, and so he starts most classes feeling behind. Even when he has completed the homework, he fails to turn it in, because he is waiting for the teacher to make a big announcement or come around to collect it. Liam feels confused all day long. By the time he gets home, he's emotionally exhausted, and when his parents complain about the mess in his room, that confusion comes out as anger toward them.

Liam needs help to identify clear, realistic goals that will improve his organization. He may need to begin by discussing what it means to be "organized" and how it will benefit him at school and at home. Liam needs guidance to set short-term goals that improve his organization (see **Prioritize** below). Each organization goal will be the building block of a new routine that needs to be created step by step. To help Liam feel successful, it's important to start small. That will require his parents to let go of some of their concerns, such as the state of his bedroom, for a little while. Since Liam needs a binder for each class, and turning in homework is an ongoing challenge, teaching Liam how to use his binder is a good place to start.

Once his binders are organized with all his loose papers filed, Liam needs to create and practice his own start-of-class routine: take your seat, take out your binder, take your homework to the teacher's desk, take out paper for notes and write the date at the top. Liam can tape a cheat sheet that lists these steps to the inner cover of the binder. His parents can ask a teacher or advisor to check in with Liam at school to see how it's going, and help him reflect on how the start of class goes when he follows the routine and when he does not. The routine will take away a minute or two of social time, so it's important that Liam can identify what he gains by giving that up.

Next, he can create an end-of-class routine: take 30 seconds to clip hole-punched paper into your binder, put other sheets into the front pocket to be hole-punched and filed that night, and note what information the teacher has given about the homework in his planner. Students can feel as if they need to rush to get to the next class, but most of time they can take a minute to wrap it up.

If they believe they do need to rush, they can take an extra minute in their next class to put away material from the previous one and then go through the start-of-class routine.

These first two steps may already improve Liam's organization and homework grade. Feeling more in control of his experience during the school day will provide more energy and motivation for Liam to complete his schoolwork at home. He will build character strengths of grit, prioritization, and self-control. Acknowledging the success he's experiencing and continuing to build on one small, clearly identified goal at a time will build a solid foundation of time and material management.

It's important to focus on one short-term goal at a time. Keep feedback related to the work on the current goal and maintaining prior goals. Comments related to the next step, chores at home, or other activities must take a back seat for now.

2. PRIORITIZE

This skill set builds on organizational skills. It means knowing what to tackle first, second, and third and includes solving problems regarding long-term tasks and assignments and managing busy school and co-curricular schedules. Planning is a key component of prioritization.

You can establish clear priorities in three steps:

1. Identify the most effective order to work on tasks.
2. Set realistic short-term goals.
3. Break up work into manageable chunks.

IDENTIFY THE MOST EFFECTIVE ORDER TO WORK ON TASKS

Young learners must balance multiple assignments, due dates, and assessments. Improving organization skills will help young learners identify priorities and know where to begin. Clear priorities, in turn, help young learners take action.

Identifying the most effective order to work on required tasks will vary depending on assignments, schedules, and personal preferences. Asking young learners to take a few moments to plan before working and a few moments to reflect afterward will help them learn how to prioritize and work more effectively.

REALISTIC AND MOTIVATING SHORT-TERM GOALS

The ability to identify and act on a short-term goal is a crucial executive function skill. Another way to think of a short-term goal is as an *action strategy*. A realistic short-term goal creates a clear priority, identifies and plans to address likely obstacles, and makes it easier to take action or get started on work. Obstacles often take the form of procrastination—resisting or avoiding the task at hand. A key to setting goals is identifying *purpose*. For example, what is this assignment teaching or practicing? What makes it worth the time? Besides supporting independence and competency, identifying purpose builds internal motivation in young learners.

TAKE NOTE

At the core, all goal-setting exercises:

- Clarify long-term and short-term goals and provide examples of realistic short-term goals that build success and motivation.
- Identify a short-term goal to take action and reflect on how to tackle likely obstacles to reaching that goal.[31]
- Acknowledge success at the completion of each short-term goal or reflect on challenges or obstacles to meeting goals. Note that obstacles are not the same as failure. Challenges completing a short-term goal mean it's time to reflect on the goal. Is it specific and realistic? Does it facilitate the change you want? What is keeping you from reaching this short-term goal? Are there ways to revise the goal to make it more motivating? Learning to reflect on an obstacle and reset a goal is a success in itself.
- Use specific and positive language—for example, *do* instead of *don't*. For example, "Complete all my English homework assignments this week" is a more empowering goal than "Don't forget any homework."

For ongoing goals—such as completing a daily chore without being asked by a parent—remember that it takes time and repetition to create a new habit.

Long-term goals take a long time and multiple steps to achieve. Short-term or action strategies are steps that can be taken immediately. Short-term goals can build toward long-term goals or fulfill an immediate requirement or assignment.

Motivating goals are specific. Many students will say that getting an A is their goal, but it is more motivating to break down the specific actions to attain that long-term goal: carefully completing each homework assignment, creating my own study guide two weeks before the next test, and reviewing my notes at the end of each week, for example. To cultivate internal motivation, it helps to review what the external motivator—or the A—represents: a mastery of the topic, effort and engagement in the class or assignment, and acknowledgement of my high level of work.

Motivating goals are also realistic. Often young learners will set such ideal goals as, " I'll do my homework as soon as I get home." But idealistic goals come with obstacles. What time does the student arrive at home? Did they attend a practice or rehearsal after school? Are they hungry, or is there a family dinner as soon as they get home? It is more motivating for young learners to think realistically about school or home expectations and then set goals they can achieve, such as:

> "I'll start my homework right after dinner, and I'll use a timer to work for 45 minutes without interruption and then take a break to check my phone."

> "I'll take 30 minutes for a snack and some downtime, and I'll set an alarm on my phone so that I begin my homework at 5 p.m."

BREAK UP WORK INTO MANAGEABLE CHUNKS

Young learners may become overwhelmed by a long-term goal or assignment, especially if they haven't used time-management strategies or procrastination has created a high-pressure situation with a looming due date. The ability to use planning strategies as soon as a long-term or complex assignment is given—to understand the tasks and break down the work into manageable chunks—is crucial to motivation and academic success. This vignette shows how failing to plan for a large assignment impacts academic performance.

Planning

Jason is a ninth-grade student studying the French Revolution. As a culminating assignment, his history teacher assigns the essay topic "Why didn't the French Revolution 'end' in late 1791? Why did it become increasingly radical and increasingly violent?" Students have three weeks to write the essay, and several classes are spent reviewing the major steps of the Revolution. Jason is not sure how to answer this essay question. He remembers part of a quote from the reading that seems like it could be part of his thesis, but he can't locate the source. The teacher says that each student needs to make an argument, but Jason isn't sure what that means. Although Jason cares about earning good grades, he continues to procrastinate when it comes to working on the history essay. Finally, the due date is only a few days away, and Jason rushes through writing a paper that does not reflect the time he spent on the reading or the energy he spent engaging in class discussions. Both Jason and his teacher are disappointed with the essay he wrote.

VIGNETTE

Jason is unable to break down the essay assignment into manageable steps. Because he doesn't understand that his job is to form an opinion and write a persuasive essay, he doesn't know how to begin prioritizing all the information he has learned. Instead, he holds on to the one idea he has for a quote to use in his introduction. When he can't locate it—instead of paraphrasing the quote the best that he can as a way to start brainstorming—procrastination sets in and he just stops.

In this case, Jason's planning failure is fueled in part by a fixed mindset approach to the assignment. He believes that he's "smart" and a "good writer," so having trouble understanding the assignment rattles him. This is where mindfulness and balance skills could help him regroup and move forward. The next step is to print out the assignment guidelines or the teacher's recommendations on starting the research and outline. Jason will benefit from reading them out loud and underlining key questions or recommendations. Then he can discuss breaking down the essay question with his teacher or parent. Jason needs to articulate his own opinion or answer to the essay question in a thesis statement. If he discusses his thoughts on the readings and class discussions early in the process, he will have had an easier time formulating his thesis.

At this point, Jason will benefit from engaging in a full writing process, instead of assuming that a "good writer" goes straight to writing the essay. Students taking a fixed mindset approach often believe they should be able to write a complete essay the first time without an outline or rough draft. But the writing process supports writers in two key ways. On one level, it helps the writer plan and execute the writing. On a deeper level, it allows for more critical thinking and connecting the dots, because it creates the space for deep thinking about the material.

Steps in the writing process:

1. Brainstorming or completing a free write.
2. Organizing ideas into an outline.
3. Writing a rough draft.
4. Revising and editing the draft.

Committing to work through these steps, Jason can schedule internal deadlines in his personal calendar that will help him use spaced practice and interleaving, allowing him to think deeply and articulate his ideas. He can complete a rough draft in time to go over with his teacher or a peer editor. Then he can revise his work to further develop and refine his argument. Working through the full writing process and seeing his ideas grow more insightful will help Jason develop a growth mindset. A growth mindset, in turn, will motivate him to put more effective and productive effort into the writing process and strengthen grit, optimism, self-control, and curiosity.

Identifying Main Ideas and Supporting Details
Identifying an effective work order, setting goals, and breaking down complex assignments into manageable chunks of work are three useful, concrete executive functioning skills. There is another, more abstract side to prioritization: the ability to prioritize information. Most notably, the ability to identify concepts—or main ideas—and supporting details.

The skill of identifying main ideas and supporting details becomes an academic expectation in around seventh grade, when developmentally students are becoming more able to engage with abstract concepts. Texts become less explicit, and students are required to infer and elaborate rather than repeat the topic sentence of the paragraph. Teachers expect students to connect the dots when reading or taking in information in class, and they expect students to do more than answer the basic question—to go a step further and provide context or analysis. In other words, deep thinking.

Students who are still fairly concrete learners will often struggle to meet these shifting academic demands. For some young learners, this is developmental and will improve in time. Some young learners lack the executive function skills needed manage the increased workload and cognitive demands. Others have excellent organizational skills but take a rigid approach to their work. In fact, these students can spend too much time over-organizing and creating "perfect" notes and not enough effort on the tiring, uncertain work of deep thinking. When schoolwork shifts away from memorizing and applying facts toward connecting ideas, expressing opinions, and creating academic arguments, a student who "can't see the forest for the trees" is going to struggle to remain engaged and productive. This vignette shows the challenges faced by a student who struggles with prioritizing the information from class and lacks the cognitive flexibility to change her approach to schoolwork.

Seeing the Forest for the Trees

After earning straight As through sixth grade, Lily is frustrated with her classes and performance in seventh grade. Her binders are perfectly organized. Her notes from class are neatly written and include all of the information from the presentations. She spends hours each night memorizing facts and vocabulary. But this year, Lily has received Bs in English, history, and science. Teacher feedback often asks for deeper analyses or examples to support her topic sentence. Lily met with her teachers, but she does not understand what she needs to do to improve her grades. Although she seems engaged and happy at school, the stress she experiences throughout the school day comes out at home. She frequently snaps at her parents, and she cries when her mother attempts to help her with her work. Lily feels exhausted most days, but she is determined to work harder and longer in order to earn As.

VIGNETTE

Lily is struggling with the changing academic expectations in seventh grade. Her work in English, history and science still require some of the study strategies that have served her so well in the past to learn the basic information. But there is a second, essential step now—Lily needs to develop her ability to identify the main ideas in the text. Once she understands the main idea, she needs to be able to connect the supporting details or relevant facts to that main idea and make connections to other topics. Lily is skilled and practiced at concrete study strategies, but she has no experience in making abstract connections, developing and expressing her opinions, or forming an academic argument. Her sense of self as a student represents a fixed mindset—she feels smart when she earns straight As. The challenges she is facing this year are creating a sense

TAKE NOTE

of insecurity and a fear that she is "not smart." Because of her fixed mindset and lack of cognitive flexibility, it is hard for Lily to try new approaches to her schoolwork.

Lily's initial reaction—to work harder and longer—is not an effective way to meet this academic challenge. For Lily, it is not about working harder. She needs to change the way she engages with the material. To do that, Lily needs feedback and guidance from a parent or teacher with whom she has a strong rapport.

In class, Lily needs to practice identifying the main idea and connecting it to supporting information—*thinking* as she takes her notes, instead of focusing on recording everything in the lecture or on the slide. Taking two-column notes on her science reading and turning her history reading annotations into two-column notes is an active study strategy that will develop this skill. (A description of two-column notes is included in Chapter 8.) After practicing this style of note taking at home, she can begin to use it in class.

Lily also needs to move away from relying on reviewing her notes to a more active retrieval practice. For example, answering the guiding questions or practice questions in the text, creating and answering short-answer questions that require her to elaborate, and teaching or talking through a lesson with a parent or peer and prioritizing the information as she presents it—starting with the big picture and then talking through the supporting details.

For writing assignments, Lily would benefit from using a graphic organizer that helps her identify for each paragraph the topic, supporting evidence, and her analysis—including her inferences and connections to related evidence.

Learning about a growth mindset can help Lily have more patience and compassion for herself as a learner and understand the importance of being open to new study strategies. For Lily, understanding the dangers of a false growth mindset is especially important.

Prioritizing Information Using Two-Column Notes

MAIN IDEA	DETAILS
WHAT IMPORTANT CHARACTERISTICS DO ALL LIVING THINGS SHARE?	CELLULAR ORGANIZATION CONTAIN SIMILAR CHEMICALS USE ENERGY RESPOND TO THEIR SURROUNDINGS GROW AND DEVELOP REPRODUCE
WHAT ARE CELLS?	THE BASIC UNITS OF STRUCTURE AND FUNCTION IN ALL ORGANISMS HUMANS = TRILLIONS OF CELLS MICROSCOPIC UNICELLULAR = SINGLE-CELLED ORGANISMS INCLUDE BACTERIA - THE MOST NUMEROUS ORGANISMS ON EARTH MULTICELLULAR = ORGANISMS COMPOSED OF MANY CELLS SPECIALIZED TO DO CERTAIN TASKS (EX. MUSCLE + NERVE CELLS)

3. TAKE ACTION!

Activation is the opposite of procrastination. Activation—or task initiation—is the skill of getting started. Specific, realistic short-term goals are great for activation.

Procrastination is a complicated challenge that is different for everyone, but it's often incorrectly assumed to be due to laziness or opposition. In fact, perfectionism is frequently an underlying cause of procrastination. This is especially true for driven, academically motivated students taking a fixed mindset approach to a subject or assignment. The pressure to meet internal and external expectations combined with challenges in time management and prioritization can paralyze even the strongest student and squash optimism, curiosity, and zest. Procrastination can also be a way that a student with a fixed mindset approach avoids taking on an academic challenge that creates a fear they will be judged as "not smart." By waiting until the last minute and rushing or cramming, they are building in an excuse for why they could not do their best work.

If a young learner is struggling with procrastination or perfectionism, understanding the individual challenges or obstacles is crucial to maintaining a strong rapport and helping them to take action. The next vignette shows the impact of rigid perfectionism on a young learner's wellbeing and performance.

VIGNETTE

Perfectionism

Mary is an eighth-grade student. Her grades started going down a little toward the end of seventh grade. But because most of her grades are still in the B+ or A- range, her parents and teachers have not addressed it. Mary spends most of the night in her bedroom "working." Really, she spends most of her time texting or online until she has to rush through her work. She believes that she can only produce work under deadline pressure, and she has gotten used to cramming for tests and staying up all night to finish essays. Her parents are concerned about her social distractions, but they are not aware of how late she stays up every night. Her teachers notice that she often looks tired, but there are no concerns about her behavior in class. Mary is stressed about her grades, and she is disappointed with most of her work. The teacher feedback on her work is consistently positive, but Mary thinks they are just being nice. She distracts herself by talking and texting with her friends, but she is not aware of how much time she spends socializing or the factors that drive her to stay plugged in for hours at a time. More and more, Mary feels like she is not good enough.

Mary is a perfectionist. Not only does she hold herself to the highest standards in all areas, but those standards may be at times unrealistic, unreasonable, or inappropriate for the goals of the task at hand. She mistakenly believes that being "smart" means producing "perfect" work the first time.

As the academic work in her classes becomes more challenging, Mary is afraid she will not be able to keep up. She is quietly having a crisis. Her sense of self is shaken, and she is afraid that her family, teachers, and friends will see that she is a fraud—that she is "not smart." All of Mary's motivation are based on one external motivator: getting an A in order to please her parents and teachers, validate her sense of self, and get into "the right college." Mary has the study skills needed to break down assignments and plan her work schedule, but the internal pressure she feels is getting in the way of her work and, more important, her wellbeing. Before addressing changes to her academic work, Mary would benefit from the intervention of a school counselor or therapist who can also provide guidance to her parents and teachers.

Learning about a growth mindset and the necessary effort and discomfort of learning may help Mary gain some insight and self-compassion and help shift her work habits. She also needs to broaden her external motivators and cultivate internal motivators. Right now, Mary sees her grades as a judgment of her self-worth. To loosen the grip of perfectionism, she needs to shift her view of grades into a less personalized reflection of effort, mastery of the material, and ability to incorporate instructions or feedback into her final product. Mary would benefit from setting internal deadlines for long-term assignments and papers and having someone at school or home review rough drafts with her to discuss her plans for continuing the work. Sharing her unfinished work makes Mary feel vulnerable. It's important to emphasize the learning process and praise her willingness to share that process.

As Mary grows more comfortable with seeing her work deepen and evolve, she will experience more internal motivators, such as a sense of pride in her work and increased self-confidence in her ability to develop her ideas—especially if she sees that it's her active engagement in the messy process of learning that makes the difference. Working in this way can help Mary strengthen her optimism and grit.

Another strategy to support Mary is to help her cultivate self-compassion and gratitude through a gratitude journal or small acknowledgments of her progress and of the people who are giving her supportive guidance and feedback. Gratitude work, like a growth mindset, is incredibly nuanced. Approached too broadly, it can backfire. Introduced with knowledge and care, a greater sense of gratitude may help Mary truly accept or take in positive feedback from others. Mindfulness exercises will also support her, since she often experiences strong emotional reactions that prevent her from accessing her strong executive function skills.

For Mary, procrastination and social distraction are ways to avoid her fear and internal struggle. Without an intervention her procrastination may worsen, and her strategy of seeking out social distraction could lead to making unhealthy social decisions. With encouragement and support to clarify her challenges and fears and strengthen activation and motivation, she can grow into a courageous, resilient learner and a more confident young woman.

Activation requires **motivation**—the desire to do things.

External motivation comes from factors outside of the self that encourage action. For young learners, this may include grades, a positive student-teacher relationship, academic success, and privileges at school or at home.

Internal motivation comes from factors inside of the self— participating in an activity that is enjoyable or feeling proud of one's work on a project or assignment. Feeling competent and confident or experiencing a sense of mastery strengthens internal motivation, grit, and zest.

When young learners earn more autonomy through thoughtful, responsible work, it boosts their internal motivation. Routines and strategies that support executive function skills allow young learners to take control of more of their responsibilities and earn that autonomy. A sense of purpose is another key component of internal motivation. If young learners understand why a task matters or how it relates to the big picture, it engages their curiosity and increases their motivation.[32]

Parents and teachers can use clear external motivators—or rewards—to help young learners build a sense of internal motivation. But it's a balancing act: Rewards can motivate, or they can become the end goal. External motivators are most effective when internal motivators are reinforced along the way—and young learners see how the time and effort applied toward achieving short-term goals pays off.

Don't underestimate an improved parent–child or teacher–student relationship as a powerful motivator. Many young learners want a strong, positive connection with the adults in their lives. Most want less stress and tension at home around schoolwork and social engagements. When young learners understand that they can earn independence through consistent, responsible actions, they will gain motivation—especially if they are receiving supportive feedback from parents and teachers along the way.[33]

TAKE NOTE

4. REFLECT

Reflection involves connecting new knowledge to background knowledge, synthesizing information and input from different sources, and articulating one's own interpretation or ideas.

Academic reflection requires metacognition—or "thinking about thinking"—and an awareness of one's personal learning strengths and challenges. It's how students connect the dots between the big picture—the concept or main ideas—and the supporting details. It helps students articulate their own ideas and arguments. Academic reflection builds cognitive flexibility—the ability to understand events or ideas from different perspectives as well as the ability to change one's strategy or approach to a task.

Personal reflection allows a young learner to understand what they are thinking and feeling. It includes self-awareness and supports metacognition and cognitive flexibility, especially the ability to understand events and ideas from different perspectives. Young learners who have the ability to reflect meaningfully are better able to manage stress, identify effective study strategies, and understand their external and internal motivators.

Young learners need practice and specific feedback in order to become skilled at meaningful reflection. Students often rush through written reflection exercises or skim the surface of the questions asked in writing or a discussion-based reflection. To strengthen the reflective skills of young learners, try pairing big-picture discussions of the benefits of meaningful reflection with pragmatic teacher- or parent-led reflections prior to and following independent student work.

Planning before working on an assignment and reflecting afterward involves creating an internal dialogue of questions in order to think about what you will do, are doing, and did. When young learners answer these self-questions, they strengthen their metacognition and cognitive flexibility.

Mindfulness skills hone reflection skills and cultivate cognitive flexibility. Practicing mindfulness also increases self-awareness and self-compassion. In turn, those qualities support empathy—the ability to understand another's experience or frame of reference. This vignette shows how a lack of self-awareness and reflection skills can negatively affect student–teacher relationships and academic performance.

VIGNETTE

Flexibility

Jonathan is in eighth grade. Although he is a hard worker and engaged in class, his grades are consistently in the mid-B range. Jonathan completes his homework and uses active study strategies to prepare for tests, but he has a habit of disregarding instructions. He jumps into the questions without reading the instructions, or he decides to do the work in a different way. On writing assignments, he frequently writes about what he's interested in, rather than addressing the prompt or question. Jonathan invests a lot of time into his work, and he's disappointed when his teachers lower his grade or ask him to redo assignments. He usually argues with the teacher to defend the way he's chosen to approach the assignment. He does not seem aware of the class time this takes up or the negative impact it has on his student–teacher relationships. His teachers are concerned that his habit of ignoring instructions will be an even bigger challenge next year in high school, when none of his teachers have a pre-existing relationship with him and there are fewer opportunities to make up work or earn extra credit.

The most common teacher comments on Jonathan's work are:

- This didn't answer the writing prompt.
- You didn't incorporate the research that we found together in class.
- Elaborate—add your own thoughts or explain it to the reader.

Jonathan consistently ignores teacher feedback, because he is not able to reflect on his work process or product. Jonathan has a lot of internal motivation for topics that spark his curiosity or interest. But he lacks self-awareness—he doesn't see when his curiosity pulls him off-topic, he doesn't think through the consequences of failing to complete the assignment as it is assigned, and he is not aware of how stubborn he appears when he argues in defense of work that does not fulfill the assignment. Jonathan has not learned how to motivate himself for a task that does not spark his interest immediately, and he has not developed an ability to reflect meaningfully on his work or his behavior.

Jonathan needs to learn how to harness his curiosity and enthusiasm and apply it toward the actual assignment. Planning and reflecting are two skills that can help him do just that. At the start of the assignment, Jonathan can allow himself time to brainstorm and take notes on his ideas on scrap paper or a brainstorming document online. That will give him space to make creative connections and voice his initial ideas. Then he needs to plan: How does this information address the assignment? What ideas from my brainstorm can I incorporate into my work? What ideas from my brainstorm do I want to save for a future assignment or an independent or creative project?

After completing the assignment, Jonathan can take time to reflect on his work:

- Did I answer the question as it was asked?
- Did I complete the assignment that my teacher created?
- Do I understand the material?
- Have I gotten off track?
- I may disagree with the instructions, but did I follow them to complete this assignment?
- What do I think the teacher wants us to learn or practice here?
- How does this assignment relate to the goals of this unit?
- What questions would I like to ask the teacher about why they chose this task or created these instructions?

Learning to have effective discussions with teachers is an important skill for young learners. Preparing thoughtful, respectful questions that show the student has already reflected on the work is a positive and productive way to begin.

When Jonathan's teachers provide feedback, he can practice listening without interrupting, asking only clarifying questions during the initial discussion. After he has reflected on the feedback, he can go back to his teacher to continue the discussion as needed. Jonathan will need help and support to develop the self-awareness and flexibility needed to reflect in an effective way. Since he has strong relationships with his teachers, he can share his goals with them and even check in to see how he's doing. He will also benefit from talking through his self-questions and discussing them with someone at home—who may even role-play the teacher—until he is comfortable with the process.

5. BALANCE—PART I: EMOTIONAL REGULATION

Emotional regulation is the ability to recognize and cope with strong emotions when they arise. This self-awareness is the first step to coping with challenges effectively. Mindfulness exercises are powerful emotional regulation tools, because they help young learners acknowledge strong feelings and take care of themselves in the moment.

Recognizing when strong feelings arise and coping with the emotional and physical effects of a stress response builds mindfulness. Mindful young learners are more able to choose how they want to respond, instead of immediately and emotionally reacting. This drastically improves problem solving, and over time it strengthens impulse control and supports overall wellbeing.

Academically, a student with high test anxiety who has the ability to identify and manage those feelings using a mindfulness strategy—such as deep breathing or positive self-talk—is more able to focus on the test itself.

Socially, a teenager who is able to acknowledge feeling nervous or awkward at a party is more able to cope with that discomfort without consuming alcohol in an attempt to feel more at ease. Adolescents with emotional regulation skills may also be better equipped to refuse offers of alcohol in a socially adept way.

6. BALANCE—PART II: EMOTIONAL MODULATION

Emotional modulation is the ability to express feelings at an appropriate volume and at an appropriate time, especially when strong emotions arise. Mindfulness exercises are powerful emotional modulation tools because they support acknowledging a strong emotion, balancing it, and consciously choosing how to best respond.

TAKE NOTE

Take, for example, a young learner who gets angry with a parent for frequently checking in during homework time. If on a scale of 1 to 10, they express that anger at a 9, then the parent's response will most likely focus on the outburst instead of the underlying feelings. If the young learner is able to voice that anger at a 6 or 7, then there is a much better chance for a productive discussion about earning more independence and privacy by regularly completing homework without social or online distractions that negatively affect the quality of the work and cause homework to take longer to complete.

Together, parent and child can create a long-term goal of independent work time with such short-term goals as "I will complete my math homework before I send any texts." They can agree on when the parent will check on the child's progress as a way to support the short-term goal. This can shift the parent–child dynamic in a positive, supportive way. (Chapter 6 includes more information and strategies for partnering with young learners.)

Together, emotional regulation and emotional modulation help young learners balance the strong emotions they experience as part of their daily lives with the executive function skills they need to work to their full potential. Emotional regulation and emotional modulation include a focus on reflection and mindfulness, and both help young learners take better care of themselves, emotionally and academically. These important skills build on the previous, more concrete executive functioning skills. It is unrealistic to expect adolescents to have the ability to regulate and modulate strong emotions if they do not have successful strategies for regulating their schedule and materials.

We can support young adults in developing these more abstract and challenging executive functions by modeling them. As parents and teachers, we need to expect that all young learners will have challenges with emotional regulation and emotional modulation. As a parent, when your child comes home in a heightened emotional state of 8—on a scale of 1 to 10—due to frustration with a teacher, grade, or social conflict, how you regulate and modulate your own emotional response is crucial. If you meet your child at 8, then the stress will escalate for both of you, and subsequent actions will likely be based on those heightened emotions.

If you are able to listen to your child but modulate your own emotional response and stay at a 4, then your child will learn that feelings can be expressed, heard, and validated without escalation. That, in turn, will help them balance—or cope—with strong feelings prior to acting.

Emotional balance skills help young learners cope with current and future challenges more independently and responsibly, both at school and in social situations.

This vignette shows one way that challenges with emotional regulation and emotional modulation can affect relationships with teachers and the entire family dynamic.

VIGNETTE

The Battle of Everything

Arthur is a ninth-grade student. He is earning mostly Cs, and his parents and teachers think he is not applying himself to his schoolwork. At home, most conversations about schoolwork or responsibilities at home quickly escalate to an argument—with raised voices and slammed doors. His parents tried "tough love" by taking away many of his social privileges, but he needs his laptop and internet access for his schoolwork. Now Arthur spends most of his time in his room, and he frequently yells at his mom or dad when they attempt to speak to him. His schoolwork has not improved, and he has become more inconsistent at completing and turning in homework.

Psychiatrist Edward M. Hallowell often tells parents, "Adolescence is the time to call in reinforcements."[34] Even though Arthur's parents have tried their best to help their son, the parent–child relationship has become strained and combative. Perhaps an extended family member or family friend can open up a dialogue with Arthur that can help him communicate more effectively with his parents. If not, the entire family may benefit from having a teen coach or behavioral therapist intervene and facilitate a healthier dialogue. (Chapter 6 provides more information about working with a coach, using a coach approach with teens, and the differences between coaching and therapy.) In either case, Arthur's parents can begin to shift the dynamic by being mindful of their own emotional modulation skills. They are increasingly frustrated with Arthur's disrespectful attitude toward them and his withdrawn, sullen affect. As a result, they frequently escalate the discussion themselves with raised voices or ultimatums. If they can do the heavy lifting of remaining grounded and calm while expressing their frustration, it will help Arthur do the same over time.

Arthur is feeling defensive and unsuccessful, but he does not know how to change his experience. He is disappointed in himself, and he cannot tolerate his parents' disappointment on top of his own. He feels powerless and "stupid," and those feelings result in him withdrawing at school and at home. Arthur does not think that he can share these feelings with his parents because of all the fighting at home. By modeling emotional regulation and modulation during their interactions with their son, Arthur's parents will become more approachable.

Behavior is often a reflection of emotions. Right now, Arthur's parents are responding to his intense emotional outbursts with their own emotional reactions. Once they lower the overall emotional reactivity at home, they can begin to address Arthur's underlying struggle through a series of short coaching conversations that will help him identify and communicate his emotions and articulate realistic short-term goals. Less tension at home, positive feedback from teachers, and improved grades are powerful external motivators for Arthur. Internally, Arthur will gain self-confidence and grit as well as emotional balance skills with each small success.

WHAT'S THE BIG PICTURE?

The vignettes in this chapter illustrate how executive function challenges can look at home and school. The interventions discussed following each vignette represent a coach approach to working with young learners. For each vignette, the interventions begin by identifying the underlying emotional struggles and the academic and behavioral challenges. Through the lenses of executive functions, mindfulness, character strengths, and a growth mindset, parents and teachers can see a more complete view of strengths, challenges, and skill deficits and create realistic short-term goals to build skills.

NOW WHAT?

Think of a few young learners in your life. What vignette or skill most relates to their challenges?

| KEY SKILLS | MINDSET | SO WHAT? | MEMORY | **CHAPTER 5 CHALLENGES** | PARTNERING | TOOLS AT HOME | TOOLS AT SCHOOL |

Identify a few strategies from this chapter that you will implement.

When and how can you model emotional balance for the young learners in your life?

HOW TO PARTNER WITH YOUNG LEARNERS TO TEACH EXECUTIVE FUNCTION SKILLS

This chapter focuses on using a coach approach to partner with young learners to strengthen executive function skills while building or maintaining a strong, positive parent–child or teacher–student relationship.[35]

WHAT IS A COACH APPROACH?

Parents and teachers value the moments when a strong rapport helps a young learner succeed—the smile when there is an unexpected moment of pure connection with a parent or seeing students light up when a lesson or discussion helps them understand a concept they have struggled with all semester. A strong rapport helps young learners meet challenges, and it can turn potentially contentious school or home experiences into opportunities to deepen cooperation and trust. That rapport is built on connection, play, practice, mastery, and recognition.[36]

Developing a strong strengths-based relationship with a young learner based on these roots is at the core of a coaching relationship. Connection creates the emotional safety that allows young learners to access their prefrontal cortex and executive function skills. It also creates the space for humor and a playful attitude in the context of working toward goals that support practice and mastery. A coach approach does not overlook challenges or obstacles. Instead, it creates a strong foundation that allows parents and teachers to use challenges or obstacles as opportunities to introduce strategies that improve organization and prioritization, identify what will help a young learner take action, and strengthen reflection and emotional balance.

Young learners often strive for independence and push boundaries. As parents and teachers, we need to see them making responsible and healthy choices. This sets the stage for a challenging time filled with parent–child or teacher–student conflict. The coach approach is a way of working together so that young learners gain independence through responsible actions while gaining important executive function skills.

WHY TRY A COACH APPROACH?

Athletes understand that you don't become your best when playing by yourself. Sports coaches help athletes assess their abilities, improve skills, stretch muscles, and strategize to prepare for high-level performance both on and off the court. By acting as executive function coaches, parents and teachers can help teens use and strengthen those skills, actively engage at home and school, and achieve their personal and academic goals.

WORKING WITH A PROFESSIONAL COACH

Chapter 5 noted the benefits of calling in reinforcements if the executive function challenges at home have resulted in increasing tension and an increasingly strained parent–child relationship. The coaching profession has grown and expanded exponentially over the past decade. Although there is currently no required credential for a "life coach," coach training and certification has grown increasingly rigorous. It is important to find the right coach for your child and family. Many coaches offer a free initial consultation, which is a good time to ask about the coach's training, certifications, background, areas of expertise, and general approach. Coaches who work with young learners often have a specific focus, although there is a lot of overlap.

We have seen the following types of coaching geared toward young learners:

- Teen coach—social, emotional, organizational, and motivational support.
- ADHD coach—attention and executive function support and parent education.
- Academic coach—executive function support, study skills, test-taking skills, and understanding changing academic expectations.

Many coaches will meet with your child in your home. A successful coaching relationship allows you step back while your child steps forward to work on short-term goals that increase independence, activation, and mastery. Many coaches focus on three main goals: self-awareness, scaffolding skills and habits, and increasing independence.

Note that coaching *does not* and *should not* take the place of therapeutic support. Many licensed psychotherapists offer coaching services, but coaching is not designed or intended to provide diagnoses, treatment, or systemic interventions for mental health disorders. Coaching focuses on the present, identifying long-term goals, and building external and internal motivation. It focuses on creating realistic short-term goals and implementing effective strategies to reach them.

In many cases, working with a professional coach can support positive, sustainable change in a relatively short period of time—often within four to eight coaching sessions. Sometimes a longer-term commitment to coaching benefits both the child and the entire family. Working with a professional coach can fast-track the use of the coach approach at home.

TAKE NOTE

USING A COACH APPROACH AT HOME OR SCHOOL

For parents and teachers, a coach approach is a way to move toward interactions with the young learners in your life. It's to help them identify and implement strategies to successfully complete assignments or tasks while strengthening key executive functions. Young learners experience a didactic approach to work most of the time at home and school—an adult provides information and then issues instructions. The coach approach encourages *dialogue* designed to increase activation, reflection, and balance.

Here are the four foundations of a coaching conversation.

1. **Focus on the present.** First, identify strengths (as discussed in Chapter 3). Then identify current challenges or work habits that are not working. Choose which specific challenge to tackle first. Keep coaching conversations short and focused on a specific assignment, task, or habit. The conversation needs to be encouraging and motivational. Avoid getting bogged down in explanations of what happened last time or idealistic plans for the future. What specific, realistic action will lead to the most effective effort right now?

2. **Identify a specific, realistic short-term goal.** If the conversation circles around a long-term goal, identify it and then refocus on a short-term goal that will take one small, solid step toward it. With each short-term success the young learner strengthens motivation, grit, and optimism. Successfully reaching short-term goals builds toward larger accomplishments. Talk with your child or students about motivation and how they can coach themselves through resistance or procrastination. Young learners often need to talk through the benefits of

TAKE NOTE

following through on an action plan and the consequences of not following through. This can be as simple as:

> "If I stick to the plan and complete my homework without going online, I will finish earlier, and I won't fight with my mom. I'll probably have time to do what I want online afterward anyway. If I spend my homework time online, it will be a more stressful night at home, and I'll end up rushing through my homework. That will hurt my grade and my relationship with my teacher."

3. **Decide how the young learner will be accountable.** When you have agreed on a short-term goal, make a plan for how you will check in together. The child could agree to check in with the parent, instead of waiting for the parent to ask—or, as they might say, nag—about it. Checking in may mean acknowledging failure. In that case, taking responsibility for not completing a goal is its own success. Reframe the conversation as an opportunity to reflect on the obstacles and set a revised goal and accountability check. Agreeing on how the parent or teacher will be involved in reaching a short-term goal creates a more positive dynamic and avoids a lot of defensiveness.

4. **Acknowledge small successes, such as meeting one short-term goal or following through on one accountability check.** Acknowledge the young learner's effort and follow-through. Remember that identifying an obstacle and creating a new goal to address it is a success in itself. When the child reaches the goal, avoid launching immediately into a list of additional tasks or assignments. Let the young learner experience the feeling of success before you engage in the next coaching conversation to identify the next short-term goal.

THE BENEFITS OF USING A COACH APPROACH

When parents and teachers partner with young learners, they help these learners gain control over their schedules and life. As a result, young learners engage more actively in schoolwork and homework. They are better able to identify feelings, express themselves in respectful and healthy ways, and communicate with peers, parents, and teachers. The coach approach establishes a working partnership and strengthens the parent–child or teacher–student relationship. It can significantly improve the quality of life at home and school as well as the young learner's internal motivation, performance, and overall wellbeing. Additionally, when you build a strong rapport based on communication and mutual respect now—with the relatively low-risk topics of organizing, prioritizing, and taking action—you open the door to honest discussions on more challenging academic and social topics down the road.

Coaching conversations help young learners internalize the questions that the coach asks. Over time, the learners become truly independent, because they can self-assess and self-adjust. This improves both academic and personal reflection, which can boost motivation and activation.

As a parent or teacher, the biggest challenges to the coach approach are staying flexible and present in each coaching conversation. It means moving away from being the expert and instead engaging in a reciprocal dialogue whenever possible. Take, for example, a common argument about playing music while doing homework. Instead of staying locked in this argument, use a coaching conversation to discuss which music styles help your child's or student's work and which can be distracting.

Of course, as an adult caring for a young learner, there will be times when you'll need to issue instructions or rules. There are many more times when flexibility is possible. In a coaching conversation, the adult leaves his or her agenda behind and creates a plan with the young learner. Hold important family or school safety boundaries, but relinquish what you assume is the right way to accomplish a task. If you disagree with your child's or student's idea, respectfully share your opinion and remain open to supporting them in trying it their own way. If it succeeds, acknowledge it. If it fails, encourage them to reflect on the failure *without judgment* or any hint of I-told-you-so.

This vignette illustrates a classroom challenge that can be addressed using a coach approach.

VIGNETTE

Speak to Me after Class

Ms. Bennett is struggling to manage the behavior of a student in her eighth-grade English class. Sonya has a habit of turning in incomplete assignments and taking up class time making excuses. She frequently distracts a few other girls by engaging them in social conversations. No single event seems significant, but taken together Sonya's actions waste class time, detract from the lesson, and encourage other students to misbehave. Ms. Bennett spoke to Sonya after class a few times, and there have been natural consequences that include lower grades and lost privileges at school. After each meeting or consequence, Sonya's behavior improves for the following class only.

Sonya is having a hard time keeping up in her classes this year. To hide her academic struggle, she withdraws academically. By making excuses for her work in front of her classmates and chatting with peers in class, she pulls attention away from her academic performance. Although Ms. Bennett intends to support Sonya's academic achievement, her meetings with Sonya do not address the underlying emotional challenges and lack of necessary skills. Sonya is unhappy about the consequences, and she modifies her behavior for class. But she quickly falls back on her covering habits.

Ms. Bennett will have more success if she switches gears and engages Sonya in a coaching conversation. She can start by identifying positive aspects of Sonya's work or participation in her class. By asking Sonya to set a short-term goal together that will build on those positive aspects, Ms. Bennett will become Sonya's partner in improving her participation in class. Shifting the focus away from Sonya's misbehavior to a short-term goal will help Ms. Bennett and Sonya create a positive working relationship. That relationship will make it easier for Sonya to admit when she is confused or not able to keep up with the work. When Sonya is able to speak openly with Ms. Bennett and receive targeted

support to address her questions and challenges, she will feel more comfortable in class.

Engaging in coaching conversations will require more of Ms. Bennett's time—at first. The payoff will be a positive student–teacher relationship, less tension and interruptions in class, and the fulfillment of helping a student gain both self-confidence and academic skills. For Sonya, the time she spends conferencing with Ms. Bennett will help her feel more connected and supported at school. That connection will help her engage more in English and other courses

WHAT'S THE BIG PICTURE?

Beginning in middle school, young learners must learn to navigate and manage their changing relationships with the adults in their lives. A coach approach offers parents and teachers a framework with which to work with young learners. It engages young learners in dialogues that improve self-awareness and articulate realistic and motivating short-term goals.

NOW WHAT?

Think of one young learner in your life. What challenges can you address with a coach approach?

- Have an initial coaching conversation focused on identifying strengths. Ask what's going well, what they feel proud of, and what they are enjoying right now—in school, as a co-curricular, or as an outside activity. Keep it short and listen more than you talk. This may lead organically to identifying challenges, or you can revisit that in the next conversation.
- Use a second coaching conversation to work together to create one short-term goal. Let the young learner take the lead. Talk through likely obstacles and strategies to succeed.
- Choose a time—maybe a few days or a week later—to follow up.

TOOLS TO TEACH EXECUTIVE FUNCTION SKILLS AT HOME

This chapter provides additional strategies for strengthening each of the key executive function skill sets at home. Since the skills overlap and build on one another, each strategy will develop multiple skills. More than any individual strategy, using a coach approach to build or maintain a strong rapport and a growth mindset will support the development of executive functions, mindfulness skills, and character strengths.

HELPING YOUR CHILD SET EFFECTIVE GOALS

Attempting to facilitate change in several of your child's habits at once often leads to frustration and increased stress at home. Follow the same guidelines for setting goals outlined in Chapter 5:

- Keep the short-term goals realistic and action-oriented. Identify likely obstacles, and make a plan to address them.
- Acknowledge small successes—which builds motivation to sustain positive change and tackle the next short-term goal.
- Use a coach approach to strengthen your parent–teen connection and help your child become more responsible and independent.

STRATEGIES TO ORGANIZE AND PRIORITIZE

Family Calendar

An effective way to model time management is to use a family calendar that shows a monthly view. Link it to your email accounts or put a physical calendar on the wall at home. Don't include everything from your child's individual calendar. Instead, stick to co-curricular and school responsibilities that affect family plans—sports games or music lessons—as well as larger tests or project due dates. Look at it with your child once a week to discuss planning and preparing for big events or big school due dates. Work backward to plan for events. For example, if you are going

TAKE NOTE

out to dinner as a family at 6 p.m. on Friday, when will your child get ready to leave?

Once you've practiced reviewing and planning with the family calendar, encourage your child to enter important dates independently.

A monthly calendar is an important tool for big-picture thinking, planning, and prioritizing. Focusing solely on individual days or one week at a time makes it easy to delay completing tasks and lose sight of the big picture. For example, a young learner who can see that each weekend in October is filled with sports games and social events will have a better understanding of how important it is for them to complete homework during the week and use Friday's study hall to work on assignments, instead of socializing.

To-Do Lists

To-do lists are tools to organize, prioritize, and take action. Keep a family or household to-do list as a way to model this tool. If you keep an electronic list, look for an app that allows for shared access. The list will be reordered and revised often.

One way to make a to-do list more motivational is to take the items on the list and turn them into short-term goals or actions. For example, instead of writing "thank you notes" on the to-do list, write "Send thank-you emails to Grandma and Aunt Laura for the birthday gifts." It may take a few more moments to add this to your list, but a clear task is easier to act on and check off the list.

For a family to-do list, add a name or initials before each item or group items by family member. For tasks that are bigger, time sensitive, or more important, add the due date to the family calendar and your child's individual calendar.[37]

Morning and Homework Routines

A strong sense of time helps young learners manage morning and homework routines. Your child will gain a stronger sense of time by paying attention to how long it takes prepare to leave the house and how much time they actually need to complete assignments thoroughly. Some people have a strong internal clock, but many people need environmental cues to help stay on schedule. Young learners do not always attend to the environmental cues available to them, and so they rely on the adults in their lives to keep them on schedule.

Here are strategies to help your child become more independent on a daily schedule.

1. Use an alarm. Ask your child to set their own alarm clock and take responsibility for getting up and moving on time.

By middle school, it is more than reasonable to expect your children to wake up and get ready independently. By making several trips to your child's bedroom room to "help" them wake up, you become the main time-management tool and probably increase the stress in your home.

Take the time to have a coaching conversation with your child about this goal. Discuss how much time your child thinks is needed to complete morning tasks and include your observations of how much time they usually take. Set a realistic time frame, and decide when and where you will check in to see how it's going each morning. An immediate benefit will likely be less parent–child tension in the morning. When your child does get moving on their own, be sure to acknowledge that success and the positive impact it had—making the morning much more pleasant for both of you and allowing your child to leave for school prepared, calm, and on time.

2. Track homework time. Ask your child to note how they spend homework time using the following strategies:

- At the start of homework time, review the assignments and estimate how much time each one will take.
- Jot those estimates down in a planner or on a sheet of paper at the desk.
- In the planner or on paper, note the time you begin and end each assignment and the time you spend on breaks or generally off-task—likely texting or online.

Don't use this information to reprimand your child or enforce consequences—the aim is to improve your child's sense of time and allow them to see when they are using time effectively or not. Young learners often underestimate how long they will need to complete assignments effectively, and most underestimate how much homework time they spend distracted or attempting to multitask. Within a few weeks, the estimates will be more accurate and help with planning. Greater awareness of the impact of electronic distractions will help young learners cultivate more discipline with their devices.

Nightly homework is a great time to practice the skills of spaced practice and interleaving, and a few minutes of planning at the start of homework time makes that possible. (Chapter 2 reviews these foundational active study strategies.) Planning adds a few minutes to the start of the homework routine, but it leads to more effective study time.

In a coaching conversation, establish how often you will check in during homework time. Remind your child that your short-term involvement is to support the long-term goal of more independence during work time. Clearly defining your involvement as a means of supporting homework goals will help avoid negative responses and tension. Look for opportunities to model mindfulness and emotional balance. If you do experience some attitude but your child is working on the goal, don't address it the moment unless you can do so with mutual humor. If the stress level in the home is rising, try taking some deep breaths and ask your child to do the same. Or try together the short mindfulness exercises at the end of this chapter.

When homework time becomes more efficient, and your child has gained back the few minutes spent organizing and prioritizing through more effective and productive work, it's time to layer on another strategy: Review.

3. Review. For each subject, encourage your child to spend five minutes reviewing previous classwork before jumping into the current assignment. One way is to have your child sum up the previous work to you as a way to check in together during homework time. Although we generally emphasize active study strategies, this is a time where the more passive strategy of review is useful. Most of the time, students jump in "cold" to new work without taking the time to connect it to the big picture. Reviewing prior to new work warms up the brain with two major benefits:

- It reinforces prior information.
- It provides useful context for the work ahead.

Healthy Routines

Young learners often have busy and unpredictable schedules. Creating routines that support balanced meals, regular physical activity, and a good night's sleep is crucial for learning and the and overall health and wellbeing of young learners.

TAKE NOTE

Nutrition: Numerous studies have documented three major ways that nutrition affects learning and academic performance.[38] First, nutrition has a major formative impact on brain function. Improving nutrition improves cognitive ability, specifically perception and reasoning. Second, since good nutrition is fundamental to good health, it leads to fewer absences from school. Third, higher-quality nutrition is associated with higher test scores. We are not nutritionists, but we consistently observe that eating healthy meals and snacks throughout the day helps young learners do their best work.

Talk to your child about what comprises a healthy, balanced meal and agree on foods that you can keep in the house to help them eat a healthy breakfast before school, snack after school, and dinner. Discuss options for lunches at school or packing lunches to bring to school. Plan dinners together, and have your child join you for the meal preparation or work on homework nearby while you prepare it.

Exercise: Research shows that aerobic exercise improves a young learners' cognitive performance—specifically performance on verbal, perceptual, and mathematical tests.[39] As noted in Chapter 4, researcher Adele Diamond has linked physical fitness specifically to executive functions. Concerns regarding the sedentary lifestyle of young learners today are well documented, and many young learners spend more time in front of a screen than moving. Sports may provide adequate physical activity during the season, but some sports do not include consistent aerobic activity.

Consider how you can incorporate aerobic activity into the time you spend with your child. Perhaps your coaching

TAKE NOTE

conversations can take place during a walk around the neighborhood. Try out hiking trails in your neighborhood. Model your commitment to physical fitness by committing to your own weekly exercise class. Finally, encourage your child to commit to several times a week when they "unplug" and get some aerobic exercise.

Sleep: It is well documented that insufficient sleep in adolescents is related to challenges in memory, learning, and performance in school.[40]

When your child was young, you had a bedtime routine—a time to wind down, clean up, do a quiet activity like reading, and generally get ready for a good night's sleep. Young learners also benefit from bedtime routines. Studies show that turning off screens 30 minutes prior to bed improves sleep—and that's a good time for your child to use for their own bedtime routine.[41] Ask your child to try the following tactics for a week, and then discuss how they affected sleep and the morning routine:

- Move electronics out of their bedroom to be charged for the next day.
- Read, listen to relaxing music, or stretch out gently.
- Use the time to shower and get materials ready for the morning.

Expect resistance to the idea of removing the phone from the bedroom. The one we hear the most often is, "But I use it as my alarm." Try a separate alarm clock that does not emit artificial light. Although the alarm function is often presented as an obstacle, we think the deeper challenge is the belief of many young learners that they must be accessible to their friends 24/7 or face dire social consequences. Often when the parent is willing to be the "bad guy," the child can "blame" you for taking the phone away at night and experience some of the benefits of unplugging—a break from social pressures, precious unmonitored time to themselves, and improved sleep. Likely, the social cost will not be nearly as high as originally feared.

STRATEGIES TO TAKE ACTION!

Cultivating effective external motivators and stronger internal motivators is an incredibly useful academic and life skill. Help young learners coach themselves by talking through the real short-term and long-term benefits of getting started on tasks, spacing out work sessions and the consequences of procrastinating. Don't underestimate your child's desire to have a positive experience with you—less stress and less arguing. Less stress at home is a great motivator for both parent and child.

Have a coaching conversation with your child, and be open to learning what they find motivational and what they know is distracting. Of course, you'll need to hold some boundaries, such as no tv or videos during work time. But you can also let your child choose whether to listen to music or work in quiet, when to take short breaks, or where to work. Encourage your child to experiment with different atmospheres to see what works best, and try working at different areas for a few days at a time. Your child will be more willing to try new routines if you model a willingness to try their idea and then reflect on the experience afterward.

Support Active Study Strategies
"You need to study!" Young learners hear this all the time, but not all young learners have learned effective, active study strategies. Instead of telling your child to "study," try asking them to tell you about an assignment and how it relates to what they are doing in class. If it's a multistep assignment or project, talk through the steps and deadlines. Encourage your child to move away from only passive study strategies, such as reviewing or rereading material, to more active work—answering questions, drawing connections, categorizing information, and practicing skills. For example, using flashcards to learn vocabulary is a bit active, but writing out sentences or labeling diagrams is a more active way to engage with the material and learn from it. (We include additional active study strategies in Chapter 8.)

You may consider committing to several sessions with an academic coach who will spend time with you and your child to review and strengthen homework routines and study strategies at home. Unlike a tutor who specializes in content support for specific subjects, an academic coach supports executive function skills and helps students strengthen study strategies, motivation, and independent work habits.

STRATEGIES TO REFLECT AND BALANCE

Increased self-awareness and flexibility will help young learners improve work habits. Improved grades are just one benefit of stronger reflection and balance skills. Other benefits are self-confidence, a feeling of accomplishment or mastery, curiosity, and zest for future work.

Meaningful academic reflection helps a young learner connect the dots by relating new knowledge to background knowledge and forming academic arguments. Meaningful personal reflection helps young learners understand what they are thinking and feeling. Reflection-based conversations can strengthen communication and your overall parent–child relationship, alleviate stress, and create more opportunities for playful moments. Use coaching conversations to practice academic and personal reflection:

- What worked—in other words, what seemed to get done more effectively?
- What was challenging? Was the challenge because it was new or different or because it was not effective?
- How did it impact the quality of your work?
- How did it lower stress? How was it stressful? What do you think it will be like next time? Was the stress related to it being new or different?
- How can this strategy gain you more time in the future?
- How can this strategy help you have a more positive experience in class or with the teacher?

Balance

VIGNETTE

Janine is a ninth-grade student. She began texting her mom, Diane, from school at 1:30 p.m., right after her English teacher returned her essay with a grade of B-. Diane decided this was an opportunity to model emotional modulation. She replied to Janine only once via text: "I'm sorry you're disappointed with your grade. Let's wait and talk this through this afternoon. I won't have access to my phone again until school is out. Love, Mom."

Later that afternoon, Diane asked Janine if she wanted to talk about the essay. As Janine began listing complaints about the teacher and the assignment, she raised her voice and her eyes welled up. Diane felt herself growing agitated toward the teacher and the assignment too, but she paused for a moment and said to Janine, "I can see how upset you are; let's catch our breath for a minute." Diane took a seat, and Janine sat down too. Diane took a deep breath and made sure her voice was at a calm, even level. She said, "It sounds like you think your grade is unfair. Let's talk about the assignment step by step." She listened to her daughter and gave occasional prompts for her to be more specific about the assigned topic and the choices she made in her work. It became clear that although Janine had put a lot of time into her writing, she had not put much time into planning. She read the assignment and formed her ideas quickly. Unfortunately, her thesis statement did not address the assignment. Since Janine did not write the assigned essay, the teacher had to lower her grade.

By guiding Janine through a thoughtful academic reflection of the assignment, Janine's mom helped her balance her strong emotional response. Modulating her own response, Diane allowed Janine to both acknowledge her disappointment and take responsibility for her errors. This process helped Janine understand her teacher's grade and made it more likely for her to remain engaged in class and learn from this experience. Although Janine applied a lot of effort writing, it was not *effective* effort. For future assignments, Janine will apply more effort to understanding the assignment and organizing her ideas *before* beginning to write.

By modeling emotional balance, Diane helped Janine feel more in control of her personal and academic experience.

STRATEGIES TO PRACTICE MINDFULNESS

All of the previous strategies to strengthen executive functions are supported by mindfulness. As discussed in Chapter 2, practicing short mindfulness exercises creates a strong foundation for executive functions by teaching young learners to take a moment to check in with their thoughts and feelings—and access their prefrontal cortex—before choosing how to respond to a situation or challenge. Mindfulness is not about imposing a calm exterior over strong emotions. It is the skill of acknowledging and balancing those emotions before choosing how to respond—and it gives young learners a greater sense of control over their experiences. Many of the following exercises that build mindfulness use relaxation techniques that also lower stress.

Your mindful presence at home is a powerful tool for teaching mindfulness. You may have an opportunity to participate in a mindfulness workshop or a training program. Mindful Schools offers the six-week online course "Mindfulness Fundamentals" that is an easily accessible place to start.[42] As discussed in Chapter 2, many forms of exercise can become mindfulness practice. Cultivating your own mindfulness will have a positive impact on your home and your child.

We believe that it is important for parents to practice mindfulness exercises themselves before teaching them to their children. Here are short mindfulness exercises you can incorporate into your home routine.

Deep Breaths
The next time stress or tension begins to escalate at home, model using deep breaths to remain mindful. You can say, "Let me catch my breath" or "I want to take a few deep breaths so I can respond with a clear head"—and then take a moment to do it.

As discussed in Chapter 2, deep breaths are a powerful tool to counter the stress response in your mind and body. Imagine you are turning the volume down on the thoughts in your head to bring your full attention to each deep inhalation and complete exhalation. Try this for three to five deep breaths, in and out. It may be hard to take a deep breath at first, because the stress response results in short, shallow breaths. After a few breaths, you may feel your breathing deepen.

Use those few breaths to regulate your own emotional reaction, and remind yourself to keep your voice at your usual level and tone. Children, even teenagers, often mirror their parents. If you are able to modulate your emotional response, your child will be better able to do the same. When you are in a dialogue with your child that becomes reactive, you can say, "Let's catch our breath for a moment. Take a couple of deep breaths with me." Ignore a low level of resistance, such as a small grimace or sigh. Your commitment to using those few breaths to shift to a more mindful dialogue will positively affect the conversation and make it easier to use again next time.

Moment of Silence

Taking a moment of silence together before beginning a meal can be a mindfulness practice. It may help to close your eyes or shift your gaze down to your plate or your lap. The goal of this moment of silence is to transition away from the stress, demands and distractions of the day to a time to connect with family. If your family says a prayer prior to having a meal together, perhaps take a few deep breaths and bring your family's full attention to the table and the prayer before you begin.

To support family members who are uncomfortable trying a moment of silence, guide your family through it at first. Here are some examples:

> "Turn the volume down on your thoughts and focus on a few deep breaths. Let out all of your air in an exhalation now and count along with me in your head. In, out. One. In, out. Two. In, out. Three. Take one deep breath on your own as you open your eyes."

> "Think about something you enjoyed today or are thankful for today. It can be big, like a person who did something kind. Or it can be small, like a good cup of tea."

> "Send kind thoughts to a family member or friend."

> "Rest in silence for a few moments."

TAKE NOTE

Mindful Hygiene

Turn the two minutes spent brushing teeth each morning and night into a mindfulness exercise. Set a goal of remaining present for the entire two minutes. Notice the taste of the toothbrush and the feel of the brush. Notice your inhalations and exhalations through your nose. Notice your posture. How does it feel to stand a little straighter? Can you relax your shoulders? When you have incorporated this into your hygiene routine, talk to your child about trying it.

Meditation Apps

Many free and low-cost apps offer short, guided meditations. Find one you like, and try out some of the exercises. Look for guided relaxation exercises that you can try with your child. Guided meditation and guided imagery are great ways to begin a mindfulness practice, because they provide a focal point that can help you shift attention away from the constant, human stream of thoughts to your breath and body in a way that can be deeply restorative.

WHAT'S THE BIG PICTURE?

Modeling the use of strategies and tools is a powerful way to teach and strengthen executive function skills. Remember that the most frustrating moments at home can be the best opportunities to model the very skills you want to help your child to strengthen. When an interaction with your child triggers an emotional response, take a deep breath. Let that mindful pause help you modulate your response by keeping your voice level and clearly choosing how to respond to the situation, rather than reacting to the disruptive behavior directly. Identify the challenge, and let your child see you solve the problem by identifying strategies to address it.

NOW WHAT?

- Remember that your child pays attention to what you do just as much as—and maybe more than—what you say. Changes you make in how you organize, prioritize, take action, reflect, and balance will have a positive impact on your child and your home environment.

Identify one or two changes you want to make for yourself as a way to model effective effort for your child:

- Getting started can seem overwhelming, especially if challenges and tension have built up over time. Set a realistic short-term goal for yourself as a parent, and acknowledge taking that first step.

Write your realistic short-term goal here:

- Use the family assessment on the next page. Use copies to guide coaching conversations and set goals together.

TAKE NOTE

FAMILY SELF-ASSESSMENT

Date _____

Review the six key executive function skill sets and identify specific skill-based challenges. Choose two skills to focus on at this time. List them in order of priority, and then identify specific strategies you will use to strengthen those skills.

SKILL SET & SPECIFIC SKILL CHALLENGES	STRATEGIES TO USE

Start with Priority #1: Have a coaching conversation to establish one or two realistic, short-term goals and commit to taking immediate action.

When will you check in together on the action plan for Priority #1? Choose a time and place to meet in three to five days.

Celebrate small successes. Success builds motivation!

© 2017 Christina Young, *Executive Functions at Home and School*. Permission to photocopy this form is granted to purchasers of this book for personal and professional learning use only (see copyright page for details).

TOOLS TO TEACH EXECUTIVE FUNCTION SKILLS AT SCHOOL

At school, we often view our students through the lens of the key executive function skill sets in the order that they are presented in this book. The more concrete skills of organization and prioritization build a solid foundation for the more abstract skills that follow. Using this lens can support students who are having a hard time adjusting to the changing academic expectations in middle and high school.

Strong students with a fixed mindset approach to learning are also likely to have limited organization and prioritization tools, because they believe they should be able to do those things in their heads. Encouraging them to use tools and strategies can free up working memory or "head space" and cultivate a growth mindset approach toward the learning process, allowing them to work deeper and stretch themselves as learners.

This chapter provides additional strategies for strengthening each of the key executive function skill sets at school. Since the skills overlap and build on one another, each strategy will develop multiple skills. More than any strategy or lesson, using a coach approach to build or strengthen rapport and a growth mindset approach will support the development of executive functions, mindfulness skills, and character strengths.

HELPING YOUR STUDENTS SET EFFECTIVE GOALS

Attempting to facilitate change in several student habits at once can lead to frustration and increased stress in the classroom. Follow the same guidelines for setting goals outlined in Chapter 5:

- Keep the short-term goals realistic and action-oriented. Identify likely obstacles, and make a plan to address them.
- Acknowledge small successes—which builds motivation to sustain positive change and tackle the next short-term goal.
- Use a coach approach to strengthen your student–teacher connection and help your students become more responsible and independent.

STRATEGIES FOR ORGANIZATION

It's beneficial to provide your students with context when using organization strategies. Take the time to review the benefits of using the tools you incorporate into class. Time spent scaffolding foundational executive function skills is gained back as students are able to work more efficiently and effectively on critical thinking tasks.

Teach your students the foundational active study strategies discussed in Chapter 2:

- Spaced practice—spacing out study sessions consistently over time.
- Retrieval practice—retrieving facts from long-term memory by using practice tests and other active study strategies, instead of rereading text and reviewing notes.
- Interleaving—*intentionally* shifting between focused work time on different subjects during each study session.

These strategies require time management and planning to implement. When you are assigning work, discuss how to use these strategies and ask students use their planners to schedule in work sessions. The book *Small Teaching*[43] explores the practical application of these strategies and outlines numerous small classroom activities that require minimal preparation or grading while boosting student engagement and understanding. Here's an example of a classroom retrieval practice.

> Mr. Taylor's seventh-grade history class is studying the legislative branch of government. For homework, they read about the House of Representatives and congressional districts. In the next class, they discuss the reading in class and then preview that night's reading on congressional redistricting. The following class, Mr. Taylor asks them to begin by answering the following questions in writing—without looking at their notes.
>
> - For what reasons were congressional districts first created?
> - What are the two most used forms of gerrymandering congressional districts? Why?
>
> After students spend about 10 minutes writing their responses, the class reviews redistricting and gerrymandering. This retrieval practice does not require prep or grading time, and it allows students to see for themselves what they understand about redistricting, and what they need to learn.

Using Planners Effectively

When used effectively, a planner is a practical organization, prioritization, and activation tool for students. Used ineffectively, it's a frustrating waste of time. Many middle schools provide paper planners, and middle school is a great time to practice using a paper planner in order to transition to successfully using an electronic planner in high school and college. Electronic planners—from utilizing an email-based calendar and task list to individual planner apps—become a practical alternative to paper planners when students are able to access their individual laptops throughout the school day. We often tell students that homework websites are for everyone, but your planner is for *you*. It's the big picture for your schedule and responsibilities, and it's your tool for working effectively and independently.

TAKE NOTE

Provide class time for students to update their planners, and periodically review them to provide accountability. Time constraints frequently result in teachers relying on homework websites, instructing students to check the site later in the afternoon. In the moment, this frees up a few minutes in class. In the long run, however it can undermine students' ability to develop key executive functioning skills. To strengthen those skills and support student independence and responsibility, use those few minutes of class to have students hear and record the assignment. Ask reflection-based questions for students to consider. This can be even more effective if there is consistency among grade-level teachers for how homework is assigned and discussed.

Depending on the assignment, you may ask questions to prompt students to think about an effective way to approach the work *before* they note it in their planners:

- How long do you think this assignment will take without distractions? Write that estimate in your planner.
- What materials do you need? What do you need to bring home today?
- What do you think is the goal or purpose of this assignment?
- How does it connect to what we're doing in class?
- What active study strategies will you use for this assignment now that you understand its purpose?
- When do you plan to work on this assignment? What else conflicts with homework—streaming videos, dinner, sports, or other co-curriculars?

A monthly calendar is a great visual aide to support time management and activation. Most paper planners include a monthly view and a weekly view. Ask students to record quizzes, tests, sports games, and weekend commitments on their monthly calendar. Students using electronic planners should look for one that allows them to view day, week, and month. Color-coding different types of events—school, homework, sports, and personal—is a useful strategy for electronic planners.

Seeing the big picture with a monthly calendar allows students to make better daily choices. For example, a student may think that homework catch-up will happen this weekend, but the monthly calendar shows a sleepover Friday into Saturday and a family event on Sunday. So that student needs to minimize online distractions this week and stay on top of homework. In high school, there are often a few quieter weeks leading up to a week of due dates or assessments in several classes. Students using a monthly-view calendar can start to predict these quiet weeks, use them more effectively to keep up with class and homework, and use spaced practice to prepare for anticipated assessments.

Class Calendar
Teachers can model effective use of a calendar by maintaining a monthly class calendar—either as a large paper calendar or an electronic calendar. Once a week, present or project the class calendar and ask the students to help you fill in your class due dates or deadlines, bigger assessments or assignments in other courses, school events, and important co-curricular events such as field trips or sports games.

Use reflecting questions to review the big picture:

- With all the events this month, how will you adjust your weeknight homework plan?
- We've just started the second quarter. What is your goal for this class for this quarter?
- When do you think tests or big projects will be announced in this and other courses? How can you use spaced practice now to prepare?

Use Intermediate Deadlines
Set intermediate deadlines for large assignments, and provide feedback on the work turned in at those deadlines. For a complex writing assignment, intermediate deadlines could be the prewriting assignment, formal outline, and rough draft. When you review the assignment and intermediate deadlines in class, provide time for students to update their planners to note the deadlines on the monthly view and plan work sessions on the weekly view.

SAMPLE STUDENT MONTHLY CALENDAR

SUNDAY	MONDAY	TUESDAY	WEDNESDAY	THURSDAY	FRIDAY	SATURDAY
Nov 1	2	3 *Home game*	4 Vocabulary quiz	5 *Away game*	6	7
8 *Family event*	9 Math quiz	10 Outline due *Away game*	11	12 *Home game*	13 Spanish quiz	14 *Service project: 9am-3pm*
15	16	17 Rough draft due *Away game*	18 Science test	19 *Away game*	20 Spanish test *Sleepover*	21 *At friend's house*
22	23 Math test	24 Final essay due	25 *No school*	26 *No school* *Thanksgiving*	27 *No school*	28 *Visit family*
29 *Visit family*	30					

© 2017 Christina Young, *Executive Functions at Home and School*. Permission to photocopy this form is granted to purchasers of this book for personal and professional learning use only (see copyright page for details).

STRATEGIES TO PRIORITIZE

Help your students see the forest for the trees. Model how to set clear priorities and help your class identify the most effective way to complete an assignment. Emphasize using each homework assignment as an opportunity for spaced practice to prepare for upcoming assessments or complete background work for upcoming projects. Remind your students about the long-term benefits of interleaving their work in your class with their work for other classes.

Planning
Teachers can model using the monthly calendar to work backward to plan study sessions. If you announce a unit test on Friday, ask students to adjust their daily homework and study plan to use effective and active study strategies starting tonight. Check in at the start of each class leading up to the test to ask if they are following through on those study sessions and how they are studying.

When you present a long-term assignment, such as a research paper, review the instructions and discuss the purpose of the assignment: How does it connect to the overall aims of the course, and what will they learn through the process? Provide time in class for students to sum up what they need to produce and think about how to get started, perhaps using a think-pair-share format—where students first take a few moments to formulate their own ideas and then discuss them with a peer before the teacher provides time for students to share a brief summary—or a written reflection exercise in class or for homework.

Sometimes procrastination begins due to a lack of clarity about the assignment or how to begin. When students are confused or overwhelmed by an assignment, they may avoid even looking at the instructions. Providing time in class for students to review the instructions and sum up their main responsibilities supports activation and motivation.

Prioritizing Information and Providing Time to Think
Another important aspect to prioritization is the ability to break down information into main ideas, concepts, and supporting details. This is a necessary skill for students managing an

increasing volume of work and increasingly abstract and multistep assignments. It is essential for determining saliency when reading complex text, analyzing evidence, and creating a thesis. Here are strategies to help students identify main ideas and supporting details in readings and during class discussions.

Create Visually Clear Instructions and Assessments

The visual-spatial layout of long-term assignment guidelines and assessments can have a big impact on student performance, and user-friendly presentation can support prioritization. Students with executive function challenges often struggle to prioritize the information or pull out the key points if the page is overloaded. Many students can feel overwhelmed when they receive a page that is packed with information or instructions, and that can lead to procrastination on projects or a stress response that affects test performance. Tuning in to how you present information visually on the page and using more space to highlight key points or providing more student workspace can improve student performance.

Encourage Active Reading

For reading assignments, model and support the use of active reading strategies. Several online active reading tools are available for free. Most active reading strategies include three steps: preview, do, and redo or reuse.

Preview

- Look for key questions included at the start or end of the section.
- Skim the section for headings, key vocabulary in bold or a separate section, and pictures or graphics.
- Identify the topic: "This reading is about _____."
- Think about how it ties in to what you last learned in class.

Previewing shows how a section or chapter is organized and can help students identify main ideas or concepts that allow them to think and prioritize the supporting details as they read. It may be helpful for the students to write a few key questions on an index card to have with them while they take the next step.

Do

- Read the section thoroughly.
- Refer to the information from your preview, especially key questions, so that you are *thinking* as you read.
- Pause before beginning a new main idea to sum up what you learned in the prior section.

Encourage students to read through a few paragraphs at a time *before* annotating. It may require more effort and time, but they will be much more effective at identifying the main idea and supporting details, their annotations will be far more useful in the long run, and there will be less need for them to reread the text.

Redo and Reuse the Information
- This is a more active last step than reviewing the reading.
- Turn annotations into two-column notes. (We include more information on two-column notes in this chapter.)
- Create a compare-and-contrast T-Chart or create a timeline of events.
- Answer the guiding and summary questions from the text or quiz yourself on the vocabulary.
- Sum up the information to yourself or to someone else without looking at the text.

The redo strategies are more active than simply reviewing the reading. Review is a useful re-engagement strategy to use prior to beginning a new reading or homework assignment or prior to the start of class.

Teach and Scaffold Note Taking
Often students are writing furiously to record what is said in class or included in a presentation without actually *thinking* about the main ideas, concepts, and supporting details. When students are not present enough to process the information in class, they often attempt to learn the material on their own by rereading their notes—usually resulting in less understanding of the material and less engagement in subsequent classes.

It takes practice and stamina to learn how to engage with the main idea and supporting information in class *and* record notes that track and clarify those ideas. It is a powerful study skill to teach to middle and high school students. The time you take to scaffold effective note taking can hugely impact your students.

Following are three strategies to scaffold note taking in class.

1. Periodically pause the discussion or lecture to provide time for your students to summarize the main ideas and supporting details in their notes. Let your students know you will do this, and ask them to put down pens or lower laptop lids and focus on listening and thinking first. This will take more time during your lesson, but the payoff will be stronger student comprehension and more student engagement.

2. Create a worksheet with essential questions or tasks. Hand out the sheet to your students to guide their critical thinking and note taking during class. Tasks can be along the lines of,

"By the next class, you will be able to answer the following questions or complete the following." At the end of class, discuss how that night's homework addresses the essential questions and tasks. Once your students are familiar with this tool, ask them to generate their own essential questions based on preview reading assignments or classwork.

3. Ask students to use two-column or "Cornell style" notes.[44] (A two-column note template is included in this chapter.) Two-column notes leave a narrow column along the left margin to record main ideas, with a wider column to the right to list supporting details. This style of note taking requires students to prioritize the information as they take notes, organizing the information in a clear, visual format:

   - At the top of the page, note the date and topic for the lesson.
   - Use a narrow column down the left side of the page to identify main ideas or concepts.
   - Use a wider column on the right for supporting details in note form.
   - At the conclusion of one broader topic, leave room to sum up the information in the student's own words, and then begin again by skipping a line and recording a new topic.

Many students we work with like taking indentation-style notes. They can still do this in the wider right column and use the thinner left column to add in main ideas or key questions. The thinner left column can also be left blank during class and used to fill in main ideas and questions in a subsequent study session. Students taking notes on a laptop can insert a table into a document with two columns—the column on the left will be narrow, and the column on the right will be wide—with multiple rows to use as a two-column note template.

Translate Annotations into Two-Column Notes

Ask students to review their reading or annotations and create two-column notes that outline the main ideas and supporting details. Often students annotate during their initial read-through, and they end up underlining what seems interesting, rather than intentionally identifying the main idea of a passage and then pulling out supporting details. Turning annotations into two-column notes will highlight that error, reinforcing reading first and then making thoughtful annotations.

Practice Summarizing the Information

When you finish presenting the information on one main idea, incorporate a retrieval practice by providing time for students to sum up the big picture in one or two sentences without using the text or their notes. You may choose to have students write this down under their two-column notes as an "exit ticket" that you review, or ask students to share their summary with a classmate. More ideas for how to use an exit ticket are included on the *Strategies to Reflect* worksheet in this chapter.

# TAKE NOTE

TWO-COLUMN NOTES

Date _____

Topic _____   Name _____

MAIN IDEA	SUPPORTING DETAILS

Sum Up: _____
_____

© 2017 Christina Young, *Executive Functions at Home and School*. Permission to photocopy this form is granted to purchasers of this book for personal and professional learning use only (see copyright page for details).

STRATEGIES TO TAKE ACTION!

Strategies to organize and prioritize address many obstacles to taking action. But many students will still need support to develop their ability to independently engage in work. Help young learners coach themselves by talking through the real short-term and long-term benefits of taking action to complete tasks and the long-term benefits of spaced practice and interleaving. Ask them to list the consequences of procrastination. Don't underestimate the desire of your students to have a positive experience in class and do their best work. These are powerful motivators!

Consistent Routines

Use consistent classroom routines for the start of class, assigning and recording homework and ending class. Knowing what to expect minimizes the distractions inherent in class transitions and helps students focus on the material you are covering.

Emphasize Learning as a Process

Make sure students know that you value the work process in your grading. Intermediate deadlines allow students to receive feedback and earn credit every time they show that they are effectively using the strategies reviewed in class. Discuss the purpose for each assignment. Foster a growth mindset approach in your students by talking about how confusion, uncertainty, struggle, and mistakes are a necessary and important part of deep thinking and meaningful learning.

Scaffold Writing Assignments

Use prewriting tasks to help students clarify the assignment, brainstorm or free write, organize ideas, and receive feedback. Value the entire writing process in your grading. Reinforce that the writer will not know at the start of the process what the final product will be—strong writing evolves through the writing process.

- Ask students to create and answer essential questions about the topics or themes, and provide time for brainstorming or free writing in class.
- Provide an outline structure or a graphic organizer for the assignment. Review the student's writing plan with him or her.

Students need clear, actionable feedback in order to improve their writing—especially in the prewriting, outlining, and rough draft stages. Create a few goals for each student's writing and focus your feedback on those goals. It can be demoralizing for a student who struggles with writing to get a lot of comments on a writing assignment.

- Encourage students to see the rough draft as a work in progress by providing teacher and peer-editing feedback, so students can see the growth in their writing with each round of revisions.

- In your assessment of the final product, refer to the student's entire writing process and how the student's work evolved through each step.

- Record your feedback on a separate page using a rubric, instead of commenting in depth on the paper. It can help to organize your feedback and highlight what the student should focus on next time. The student can review the rubric again before beginning the next writing assignment and set a few goals for their writing.

Support Active Study Strategies
"You need to study!" Middle and high school students hear this all the time, but not all young learners have learned effective or active study strategies. Passive studying includes reviewing or rereading material, whereas active studying includes the foundational strategies of spaced practice, retrieval practice, and interleaving to support asking and answering questions, making connections, and practicing skills over time.

- When you announce a quiz or test, take time to review your recommended active study strategies with the class.
- Instead of telling students to use their homework time to study, assign a specific, active task, such as creating and answering short-answer questions—or provide a practice test.

If you have parent education events, consider using some of that time to review active study strategies with parents so they know how to encourage their children at home. More specific active study strategies are listed on the *Active Study Strategies* resource sheet in this chapter.

TAKE NOTE

ACTIVE STUDY STRATEGIES

TEACHER-PROVIDED STRATEGIES

Provide blank copies of homework, quizzes, or tests for students to redo.

Provide blank copies of maps or diagrams for students to label.

As a class activity, create a timeline that illustrates the causes and effects of events.

Give practice quizzes for retrieval practice. Correct the quiz in class and have students use it as a study guide.

Create a pretest reflection worksheet. Ask students to sum up the big picture. If they were giving this test, what would they assess? Why would they choose that? For example, why is a specific date important? A person? An idea?

Ask students to reflect on the study strategy they used after an assignment is complete:
- How much extra energy or effort did it require?
- What was the payoff for you as a student?
- How did it affect class or homework time at home?
- Where else can you use this active study strategy?

STUDENT-CREATED RESOURCES

Use your planner to schedule spaced practice sessions.

Turn annotations into two-column notes.

Create and answer practice short-answer questions or word problems (with an answer key). Swap with a classmate for practice.

Teach the material to someone at home. Reflect on what was successful and what was challenging about the experience.

Create mnemonic devices to remember important information, items in a series, or parts of a diagram—use acronyms, keywords, visuals, songs, or rhymes.

Create a student study guide as soon as a test is announced. Compare it to the teacher-provided study guide.

Annotate teacher-provided study guides: check only what needs review, circle what needs practice, and star what needs to be relearned or reviewed with the teacher.

Write major concepts or themes on chart paper to hang on the wall. Relate different events or concepts to them.

Go beyond flashcards! Write sentences that show the meaning of the words. Practice using the words in conversation. Label items at home.

© 2017 Christina Young, *Executive Functions at Home and School*. Permission to photocopy this form is granted to purchasers of this book for personal and professional learning use only (see copyright page for details).

TAKE NOTE

PRETEST SELF-REFLECTION

Name _____   Date _____

Course _____   Unit _____

Review homework assignments, notes, and readings to determine your current level of proficiency with each topic.

Fill in the chart by listing main topics in order and checking the box that best describes your understanding of the topic.

MAIN IDEA	STRONG *Could teach to someone.*	OK *Need more practice.*	SHAKY *Need to review notes, watch videos, or get help.*

Look at the OK and Shaky columns:
1. For the topics that need practice or help, select challenging questions or problems from previous work.
2. Write out the selected questions or problems and redo them, elaborating in your response or showing all your work.

For the topics you need help to understand:
1. See what resources you can use independently.
2. Take your questions and the work you've done to a meeting with your teacher.

© 2017 Christina Young, *Executive Functions at Home and School*. Permission to photocopy this form is granted to purchasers of this book for personal and professional learning use only (see copyright page for details).

STRATEGIES TO REFLECT

Meaningful academic reflection helps young learners connect the dots by relating new knowledge to background knowledge, making connections and forming academic arguments. Meaningful personal reflection helps young learners understand what they are thinking and feeling. Bringing more academic and personal reflection into your classroom helps students engage with the material. That boosts motivation and activation as well as such character strengths as grit, curiosity, and optimism.

Reflecting effectively creates an interior dialogue of questions and responses in the learner about what they will do, are doing, or did. This increased self-awareness helps students partner with teachers to improve work habits.[45]

Feedback is key to teaching reflection. Students may not accurately gauge what is helpful or not helpful at first. Often a task that is effortful is incorrectly categorized as unhelpful, while a more passive task that does not require deep thinking feels easier and is incorrectly categorized as helpful. That may explain why many of our students swear by Quizlet for memorization but resist using the more effective strategies of writing out sentences or more effortful and effective recall practices. It's important to help young learners differentiate between what seems easy and what is effective.

Written Reflection Exercises

To strengthen your students' ability to reflect, begin with written reflection exercises to build the norms for reflecting in your class. When your class has practiced reflection in writing, try a reflecting discussion in class using the same clear guidelines as those used in written reflections. Try reflecting on the foundational executive function skills you are building in class. You can use the *Note Taking Reflection* worksheet included in this chapter to review the purpose of prioritizing and thinking while taking notes. Teacher-provided feedback will be a key part of this reflection.

As your students grow more skilled at reflecting, incorporate student feedback in your classroom routines and assignments. Ask students to reflect on the class environment, and reward meaningful reflection by implementing small changes based on their feedback.

Teach Goal Setting
Goal setting is discussed in Chapter 5, and many goal-setting exercises are available online. Providing class time to review how to set realistic, motivating short-term goals that support long-term goals introduces the vocabulary of goals into your classroom. Then you can use goal setting as a way to strengthen planning, activation, and reflection skills. As a reflection exercise, ask students to set goals for the quarter or semester, or provide time for them to write a goal statement on an assignment sheet or study guide.

Transition To and From Class
Consistent exercises at the start and end of class can create a smooth transition to class and cultivate reflection skills. Many teachers begin class with a bell ringer or do now assignment for students to work on as soon as they enter the room. This exercise can help students settle in and focus on class, even as other students are still entering the room. They can be used to practice retrieving information from the previous class, highlight a theme for the present class, or provide an opportunity for students to ask or answer guiding questions.

An exit ticket is an activity at the end of class that provides an opportunity for students to sum up the main idea from class or articulate their own thoughts or arguments. Exit tickets can be collected as students leave or answered in student notes and reviewed by the teacher in class. Entrance tickets and exit tickets help gauge what needs review in a class versus what has been mastered by many.

TAKE NOTE

REFLECTION EXERCISES

Provide class time to help your students review long-term assignments and plan a work strategy. Ask them to sum up their main responsibilities in a few sentences.

On your review sheets, provide a space to reflect on any errors they made during the review practice, and then ask students to write a goal statement to prepare for and take the test.

When assignments are turned in, take some class time to reflect on the process. What went well? What was challenging? How would they work differently next time?

Review and reflect on graded assessments. For example:

- Conduct an error analysis on a math quiz and discover that many errors were related to computation errors.
- Set a goal for next time to check computations twice before moving to the next problem.

Reinforce that improved grades are just one benefit of stronger skills and work habits. Other benefits include mastery, improved quality of life at school, and improved self-awareness and self-confidence.

When you look out and see a lot of sleepy faces, ask your students to stand and stretch before continuing class.

Ask students to write their own teacher comments before they receive a report from school. If possible, use some of their insights for your own student comments. After students receive your comments, ask them to complete a reflection or goal-setting activity based on their comments.

Use this space to create questions that will help your students reflect on a recent assignment.

© 2017 Christina Young, *Executive Functions at Home and School*. Permission to photocopy this form is granted to purchasers of this book for personal and professional learning use only (see copyright page for details).

TAKE NOTE

NOTE TAKING REFLECTION

Name _____ **Date** _____

Think about a time you took notes in class that turned out **not** to be helpful when it was time to use them to complete an assignment or study for a test. Describe the style of notes you took. Did you ever put your pen down during the class? What about your notes were **not** helpful?

_____

_____

_____

_____

_____

_____

Think about a time you took notes in class that turned out to be helpful when it was time to use them to complete an assignment or study for a test. Describe the style of notes you took. Did you ever put your pen down during the class? What about your notes were helpful?

_____

_____

_____

_____

_____

_____

TAKE NOTE

ERROR ANALYSIS FOR MATH
How to Reduce "Careless Errors"

Step 1: Identify the Type of Error

Most errors are not due to a lack of caring. Here are six common mathematical errors.
For each wrong answer, find out where you went wrong. What didn't you do or know when you answered this question?

1. **Computational**—Did you make a mathematical calculation mistake?
   Example: You wrote that 2 + 3 = 6.

2. **Conceptual**—Did you not understand the mathematical process or theory?
   Example: You did not line up the decimal points when adding decimals.

3. **Reading**—Did you misread the directions and answer with something not asked for?
   Example: You found the perimeter when the directions asked for the area.

4. **Omission**—Did you forget important information even though you completed the work correctly?
   Example: You forgot to include the units, or you forgot a solution sentence.

5. **Presentation**—Did you follow the proper format?
   Example: You did not show every step, or your work was unclear.

6. **Copying**—Did you make a mistake copying from one line to the next?
   Example: You wrote a negative sign for a number, instead of using the positive sign from the line above.

Step 2: Correct the Error

Redo the problem from beginning to end. This is an effective way to avoid the same error on future tests. Complete your corrections on lined paper using the following steps:

- Rewrite the problem and write what type of error you made.
- Write out the specific error and how many points you lost.
- Solve the problem correctly and show all of your work.

$$\frac{a}{3a+1} - \frac{4a-7}{9a+3}$$

$$\frac{3a}{9a+3} - \frac{4a-7}{9a+3}$$

$$\frac{3a - \boxed{4a-7}}{9a+3}$$

$$\frac{-a-7}{9a+3}$$

ERROR: WHEN SUBTRACTING BINOMIAL IN RATIONAL EXPRESSION NEED TO "SUBTRACT" ENTIRE TERM
→ CONCEPTUAL ERROR

CORRECTION:

$$\frac{a}{3a+1} - \frac{4a-7}{9a+3}$$

$$\frac{3a}{9a+3} - \frac{4a-7}{9a+3}$$

$$\frac{3a - (4a-7)}{9a+3}$$ CORRECT PROCESS

$$\frac{3a - 4a + 7}{9a+3}$$

$$\frac{-a+7}{9a+3}$$

© 2017 Christina Young, *Executive Functions at Home and School*. Permission to photocopy this form is granted to purchasers of this book for personal and professional learning use only (see copyright page for details).

TAKE NOTE

STRATEGIES TO BALANCE

When young learners strengthen their ability to cope with strong feelings and express themselves in a way that leads to productive dialogue, the student–teacher connection becomes stronger. That student is now able to work through the challenges inherent in learning with less frustration, and there is more opportunity for playful moments.

Prepare for Student–Teacher Meetings
Teach students how to prepare for individual meetings with teachers and emphasize the importance of scheduling a meeting to discuss concerns, rather than blurting them out in class. Review the components of an effective student–teacher conference:

- Prior to the meeting, the student reviews the material and prepares specific questions.
- The student begins by stating their concern and reviewing the work process and challenges. Arguing over a grade is not an effective way to address concerns.
- The student is prepared to end the conference without receiving an answer or the answer they want. You are building a strong student–teacher relationship that will be helpful all year.

Teach students how to cope with stressful experiences in the classroom:

- If you are experiencing an intense emotion, take a few deep breaths before raising your hand or speaking out.
- If that pause does not balance the emotion, that is a cue that you should wait and speak to the teacher individually after class instead of speaking out in class.
- Try discreet mindfulness exercises to cope with intense emotion. For example, with your hands on your lap, take a deep breath in and gently squeeze your fists. On a full breath out, relax your hands. You can do this one hand at a time and then with both hands together for a total of three deep breaths. Alternatively, you can take a deep breath in and make a fist

with one foot inside your shoe, and then on a full breath out relax the foot and repeat on the other side.

Teachers can facilitate emotional balance by clearly establishing guidelines for discussing grades. Establish these guidelines, and practice holding conferences on lower-stakes quizzes and assignments before your next big assessment.

- Give students an opportunity to discuss grades when they are returned, ideally the same day.
- Provide 10-minute student–teacher conference appointments in class, during lunch, or after school. If students have practiced preparing for conferences, they can use those 10 minutes effectively to voice their concerns.
- Let students know that you will listen to their concerns and provide an answer the following school day, after you have time to reflect on the conference and the student has time to reflect on their effort, performance, and grade.

Establish a Vocabulary for Emotional Modulation

The *Express Yourself* reflection worksheet included in this chapter is designed to teach students about emotional modulation. Once your students have practiced balancing and modulating emotions in school, you can ask balancing reflection questions in class, such as, "What volume are you speaking at right now?"

Here are a few ideas for alternative exercises to teach emotional modulation:

- Create a gauge from 1 to 10, and ask students to mark where their feelings would be in various situations.
- Create a thermometer measuring from cool to hot, and ask students to mark their "temperature" in various situations.
- Ask students to create their personal weather report—for example, "Cloudy with a chance of rain," "Thunderstorms," or "Sunny and warm."

If students report strong emotions, ask how they can take care of themselves and stay present at school.

 **TAKE NOTE**

REFLECTION — EXPRESS YOURSELF!

Name _____ **Date** _____

Imagine you are a speaker with volume levels from 1 to 10. When you feel a strong emotion, at what volume are you likely to express that emotion?

How will your teacher respond to expressing yourself at that volume?

How will a parent respond to expressing yourself at that volume?

Will you be able to address your concern, hurt feeling, or question after expressing yourself at that volume?

What is the highest volume that you think your teacher or parent can hear and still address your concern, instead of addressing how loudly you are sharing that concern?

What can you do to take care of yourself enough to be able to lower the volume that you are using to share your concern?

© 2017 Christina Young, *Executive Functions at Home and School*. Permission to photocopy this form is granted to purchasers of this book for personal and professional learning use only (see copyright page for details).

STRATEGIES TO PRACTICE MINDFULNESS

All of the previous strategies to strengthen executive functions are supported by mindfulness. As discussed in Chapter 2, practicing short mindfulness exercises creates a strong foundation for executive functions by teaching young learners how to take a moment to check in with their thoughts and feelings before choosing how to respond to a situation or challenge. Mindfulness is not about imposing a calm exterior over strong emotions. It is the skill of acknowledging those emotions and balancing them before choosing how to respond—giving young learners a greater sense of control over their experiences. Many of the exercises that build mindfulness use relaxation techniques that also help lower stress.

Your mindful presence in the classroom is a powerful tool for teaching mindfulness. You may have an opportunity to participate in a mindfulness workshop or a training program as part of professional development. You'll find a wide range of free and low-cost meditation apps you can use to try out some of the exercises. As discussed in Chapter 2, running, yoga, and other forms of exercise can become a mindfulness practice. Cultivating your own mindfulness will positively impact your classroom and your students.

We believe it is important for teachers to have experience practicing mindfulness exercises themselves before asking students to try them.

Here are some mindfulness exercises to begin or end student work.[46] Students can participate at their desks with their materials out, or you can ask them to close books or flip over papers that are a distraction. Keep the transition from these exercises to your classwork relatively quiet and still. Give instructions slowly and calmly in a natural voice. Provide a clear transition from the mindfulness exercise to the start of classwork.

Mindful Posture

Middle and high school students frequently slouch. We are not opposed to slouching. In fact, in our experience some students need to fidget or slouch to stay engaged. Mindful posture is not meant to enforce sitting up straight for an entire class. Instead, it's a mindfulness exercise that gives students an opportunity to see how posture and body language can affect experience. Some students may find that maintaining a mindful posture throughout class is beneficial for their learning. Others may find shifting into a mindful posture for a few moments a way to re-engage in class or return their attention after a distraction.

TAKE NOTE

Mindful posture is not rigid—it's just more engaged and self-aware. Here's an example of how you can guide students into a mindful posture:

- Sit up straighter for a few moments, and take deeper breaths in and out.
- Uncross your legs and put both feet on the floor.
- Rest your hands on your desk or your lap.
- Let your shoulders drop away from your ears.

Provide a clear transition back to classwork—for example, "You can choose to stay like this or gently shift in your seat. We'll begin class now."

Teach mindful posture a few times, and you can refer to it in the future to start a mindful breathing exercise or as a mindful check-in during class. For example, say, "The energy in here is really low—everyone shift into a more mindful posture for a few moments and let's see if this change in posture changes anything." Here are some reflection questions for mindful posture:

- How much more effort does it take to have a mindful posture? What do you gain?
- Are there small adjustments that you can make so that your body language shows you are getting ready to work and bringing your attention to the current moment?

TAKE NOTE

Mindful Breathing and Moment of Silence
These mindfulness tools can help students transition from any hectic and stressful experiences in the day to your class.

Mindful Breathing: Take a break for a few deep breaths. Make this part of your routine at the start of class or when you can tell by body language that their attention or stamina is waning. Some students may be uncomfortable trying it, and others may end up thinking more about stressors during the exercise. Provide guidance regarding what to focus on while taking deep breaths:

- Shift into a more mindful posture.
- Close your eyes if that's comfortable, or keep your gaze at your desk or the floor in front of your desk.
- Breathe in quietly, through your nose if that's comfortable, and pay attention to the full breath in. What parts of your lungs and torso expand with the breath?
- Breathe out quietly, through your nose if that's comfortable, and pay attention to the full breath out.
- Turn the volume down on your thoughts and bring your attention to the quiet sound of your inhalation and exhalation.

Provide a clear transition—for example, "Please open your eyes. We'll begin class now."

Moment of Silence: Incorporate a moment of silence into your routine at the start of class. Share with students that you intend to use a moment of silence to transition from the previous activity of the day to this class and this lesson. If your students seem distracted in class, a moment of silence mid-class can help refocus. For some students, silence is challenging. Let students know that they will not be asked to share any of their thoughts or images from this exercise. Provide guidance during this exercise:

- Shift into a more mindful posture.
- Close your eyes if that's comfortable, or keep your gaze at your desk or the floor in front of your desk.

- Notice each breath in and out.
- Turn the volume down on your thoughts. *Or,*
- Think of something you are grateful for today. It can be something big or something small. *Or,*
- Picture your favorite place in nature—for example, a beach or a mountain trail. Notice the colors, the textures, and the sounds.

Provide a clear transition—for example, "Please open your eyes. We'll begin class now."

Take a Break

For middle school students, one way to introduce mindfulness is to take a break at the start of class once or twice a week. At first, you may allow students to put their heads down on their desks. Turn down the lights, and give them a few minutes to do nothing. When this is part of your class routine, you can ask them to practice in a mindful posture. Let students know that they will not be asked to share any of their thoughts or images from this exercise. Provide some guidance:

- Let's start by taking three deep breaths together. Exhale now and we'll begin. In, out. One. (Continue to three.)
- Now take a few moments to rest and notice what thoughts come up in your mind. Just notice the thought, and then bring your attention back to your breath. *Or,*
- Picture your favorite place in nature—for example, a beach or a mountain trail. Notice the colors, the textures, and the sounds. *Or,*
- Take some quiet, deep breaths. With each quiet exhalation, let out a little stress or tiredness.

Provide a clear transition—for example, "We'll begin class now. Please open your eyes."

Mindful Moment

When you observe that your students are growing distracted, frustrated, or extra fidgety, share your observation in a neutral, nonjudgmental way and lead a mindful moment:

- Stand and stretch. *Or,*
- Put down your pencil, make fists, and then release or shake out your hands. You can coordinate this with your breathing by inhaling when squeezing your fists and then exhaling when releasing your fist and gently wiggling your fingers. *Or,*
- Ask students to silently identify what they are thinking about and how they are feeling, and then ask them to shift their focus back to the classwork.

End with a Guided Reflection

At the end of class, lead a short, silent reflection. You may choose to begin with a moment of silence or a short deep-breathing exercise. Then ask students to think of something from the class that stood out—an aha! moment or something they want to remember. This can be the time they use to sum up the main concepts from the lesson before writing an exit ticket. Or ask your students to identify for themselves the actions they need to take between now and the next class, and provide a few minutes for them to note a study time and goal in their planner.

WHAT'S THE BIG PICTURE?

Taking class time to teach and practice executive function skills will pay off in greater student comprehension and increased student engagement. Remember that the most frustrating classes can be the best opportunities to model the skills you want to help your students strengthen. Rather than attempting to forge ahead when you observe that your students are distracted or disengaged, pause for a moment to take a deep breath. Let that mindful pause help you modulate your response by keeping your voice level and clearly choosing how to respond to the situation in a way that restores the classroom to a learning environment, rather than reacting to or ignoring the disruption. Identify the challenge, and let your students see you solve the problem by identifying strategies to intervene.

WHAT NOW?

- Remember that your students pay attention to what you do just as much as—and maybe more than—what you say. Changes you make to organizing, prioritizing, taking action, reflecting, and balancing will positively impact your students.

Identify one or two changes you want to make for yourself and as a way to model effective effort for your students:

- Getting started can seem overwhelming, especially in the middle of a busy school year. Set a realistic short-term goal for yourself as a teacher, and acknowledge taking that first step.

Write your realistic short-term goal here:

- Remember that the effort you put into creating this new dynamic with your students will pay off in a positive, supportive, productive class environment.

 **TAKE NOTE**

SKILLS FOR STUDENT SUCCESS

ORGANIZE
- Use a planner—a monthly view for big events and a weekly for homework.
- Set your own alarm clock and get up on your own in the morning.
- Keep a clock—not your phone—where you do your homework. Keep track of how much time you spend on each subject and how much time you spend off task.
- Keep binders tidy—hole-punch and file papers during homework time.
- Put the date and topic on all notes.
- Make a plan with your parents. When will they check in?
- Eat something healthy with breakfast, lunch, and dinner.
- Include sleep in your time-management plans.

PRIORITIZE
- Take a few minutes to decide what to do first, second, and third *before* you start your work.
- Think and talk through your plan for completing each step in long-term or complicated assignments.
- Practice active reading and use two-column notes.

TAKE ACTION!
- Remind yourself of the benefits of getting to work and the consequences of putting it off or not doing it.
- Take out all the materials you need and sit in front of them for 10 minutes without going online or using your phone.
- Work on one thing that it will feel good to accomplish.

REFLECT
- What is this assignment intended to practice or teach?
- What do you gain by completing this assignment thoughtfully?
- What active study strategy can you use?
- When an assignment is returned, review it. What have you learned since this assignment? How can you improve your work on future assignments like this one?

BALANCE
- Take a few deep breaths when you experience a strong emotion *before* you say or do anything.
- Practice deep breathing and other mindfulness exercises.
- Create a relaxing 30-minute bedtime routine with no electronics.
- Imagine your emotions on a speaker with the volume from 1 to 10. At what volume will your concerns be clearly heard?

© 2017 Christina Young, *Executive Functions at Home and School*. Permission to photocopy this form is granted to purchasers of this book for personal and professional learning use only (see copyright page for details).

9 CONCLUSION: PUTTING IT ALL TOGETHER

Parents and teachers want the best for the young learners in their lives. They want to see those young learners "work hard," "act responsibly," and "be happy." We believe that young learners are acutely aware of those hopes *and* expectations and that those general, long-term goals *do not* help them to succeed any more than telling them to "study" helps them use effective strategies to learn.

We believe that what *does* help young learners is—first and foremost—a strong rapport with parents and teachers built on communication and mutual respect. That relationship is cultivated by acknowledging strengths, identifying challenges, creating specific and realistic short-term goals, taking action, reflecting on results, and balancing emotional responses. To that end, we use several lenses to view the young learners in our lives.

Executive functions are the primary lens we use. Understanding the key executive function skill sets for young learners allows us to identify strengths and challenges—or skills and skill deficits—and teach the strategies and tools that will best support them.

Mindfulness is the second lens. We view mindfulness as a powerful and necessary foundation for executive functions. The ability to acknowledge strong emotions and choose how to respond—rather than immediately react—allows young learners to access their executive function skills and apply them to real-life challenges.

Character strengths and a **growth mindset** comprise the third lens. We see these as personal attributes that can be developed through conscious actions—and, in our experience, they support strong executive function skills.

We have shared these lenses with you because going straight at an academic challenge in isolation is rarely successful. Taking a good look at these three overlapping domains provides an important view of the whole young learner. Use that perspective to identify specific challenges, prioritize which ones to work on first, and engage your child or student in a productive dialogue.

As this book illustrates, there are often developmental or personal challenges underlying the academic ones. When a young learner feels seen and heard in a respectful way, they will be more able to take an honest look at what needs to change and commit to using new strategies and tools to meet the challenge. Working this way, you will build a stronger personal connection and strengthen your child's or student's self-awareness and overall wellbeing. We strongly believe those gains will positively impact that young learner for the rest of their life.

ENDNOTES

See References section for full citations.

---

[1] See Laurence Steinberg's *Age of Opportunity: Lessons from the New Science of Adolescence.*

[2] See Laurence Steinberg's "A Social Neuroscience Perspective on Adolescent Risk-Taking."

[3] Psychologist and neuroscientist Joanne Deak's work addresses the significance of research illustrating that the amygdala swells during adolescence. See Deak's *How Girls Thrive*. Laurence Steinberg also articulates the developmental mismatch between the prefrontal cortex and the amygdala in *Age of Opportunity*.

[4] Adele Diamond, Ph.D., FRSC, is a prominent figure in developmental cognitive neuroscience. She has published and presented extensively on executive functions. Diamond identifies working memory, inhibitory control, and cognitive flexibility as three core executive functions. For information on her research that documents the importance of social, emotional, and physical health on executive functions, refer to www.devcogneuro.com.

[5] Herbert Benson, M.D., defines the relaxation response as "the physical state of deep rest that changes the physical response to stress . . . and the opposite of the fight or flight response." In *The Relaxation Response*, he describes how to use deep breathing techniques to achieve this response.

[6] Find more information about Jon Kabat-Zinn, Ph.D., and the history of MBSR at the UMass Center for Mindfulness in Medicine, Health Care, and Society, at www.umassmed.edu/cfm.

[7] The Linehan Institute offers more information about DBT at www.linehaninstitute.org. Learn more about research on MBCT at the National Center for Biotechnology Information at www.ncbi.nlm.nih.gov.

[8] See Ellen Langer's *The Power of Mindful Learning*.

[9] Learn more about the history of mindfulness in education and research and training for parents and teachers at Mindful Schools at www.mindfulschools.org.

[10] Charlotte Zenner, Solveig Herrnleben-Kurz, and Harald Walach detail this evidence in the 2014 article "Mindfulness-Based Interventions in Schools—A Systematic Review and Meta-Analysis."

[11] Learn more at www.characterlab.org.

[12] Character Lab is a nonprofit organization founded in 2013 by Angela Duckworth, a MacArthur Fellow, and Christopher H. Browne, Distinguished Professor of Psychology at the University of Pennsylvania; Dave Levin, co-founder of the KIPP public charter schools; and Dominic Randolph,

head of Riverdale Country School. In 2016, Character Lab moved its headquarters from New York City to the campus of the University of Pennsylvania.

[13] Learn more about the VIA Classification of Character Strengths and Virtues at www.viacharacter.org/www/Character-Strengths/VIA-Classification.

[14] In *Smart but Scattered*, school psychologist Peg Dawson and psychologist Richard Guare define goal-directed persistence as an executive function skill that refers to the ability to set goals and work toward them without becoming sidetracked by competing interests. We view goal-directed persistence as closely related to grit and to our key skill set Take Action!

[15] Psychologist Daniel Goleman's book *Emotional Intelligence* posits that IQ and academic knowledge is just one criteria of personal, academic, or professional success. Other necessary criteria are self-awareness and an awareness of others. Goleman identified the five domains of emotional intelligence.

[16] Psychologist and researcher Carol Dweck's book *Mindset*, based on empirical evidence, defines both fixed mindset and growth mindset and explores the benefits of cultivating a growth mindset. In school settings, she measured students' mindsets as they entered middle school. Students with fixed mindsets showed a decline in academic achievement over two years as academic expectations and challenges increased; students with growth mindsets showed an increase in grades over two years.

[17] Learn more in Carol Dweck's 2016 article "Recognizing and Overcoming False Growth Mindset" at www.edutopia.org/blog/recognizing-overcoming-false-growth-mindset-carol-dweck.

[18] In *Make It Stick*, Peter Brown, Henry Roediger III, and Mark McDaniel review the science of deep and durable learning and the positive impact that effective learning strategies make in both educational and professional settings.

[19] John Dunlosky covers effective learning strategies in his 2013 article "Strengthening the Student Toolbox."

[20] See John Dunlosky's "Strengthening the Student Toolbox."

[21] See Joshua Rubinstein, David Meyer, and Jeffrey Evans' 2001 article "Executive Control of Cognitive Processes in Task Switching."

[22] A useful article outlining the costs of multitasking and ways to avoid it can be found at www.psychologytoday.com/blog/brain-wise/201209/the-true-cost-multi-tasking.

[23] The American Psychological Association offers this and many other resources online at www.apa.org.

[24] Psychologist Lynn Meltzer, president and director of research at the Institute for Learning and Development, outlines memory processes in her book *Promoting Executive Function in the Classroom*. See also Adele Diamond's studies and information at www.devcogneuro.com.

[25] Daniel Willingham discusses the biological and cognitive basis of learning in his 2009 book *Why Don't Students Like School*.

[26] Psychologist Laurence Steinberg's research documents how a sense of connection and support increases learning. See Steinberg's *Age of Opportunity*.

[27] See David Yeager, Gregory Walton, and Geoffrey Cohen's 2013 article "Addressing Achievement Gaps with Psychological Interventions."

[28] Psychologist Russell A. Barkley's extensive research on ADHD specifies five discrete skills a young learner must be able to use in order to "pay attention." See Barkley's *Taking Charge of ADHD*.

[29] In 2010, researcher Diane M. Bunce and her colleagues studied the adolescent attention span. Their published results document a pattern of frequent attention lapses in teenage students that usually last one minute or less. A common pattern was a lapse within the first 30 seconds of a lecture, followed by brief lapses every four to five minutes. The lapses became more frequent as the 50- to 90-minute lecture progressed, eventually occurring every two minutes. See their article "How Long Can Students Pay Attention in Class? A Study of Student Attention Decline Using Clickers."

[30] Adele Diamond's discusses the impact of sleep and physical fitness on executive functions in her PDF "Executive Functions" at www.devcogneuro.com/Publications/ExecutiveFunctions2013.pdf.

[31] Gabriele Oettingen's "WOOP" planning action strategy emphasizes the importance of thinking about likely obstacles in the planning stage of goal setting. Learn more in her book *Rethinking Positive Thinking* and at www.woopmylife.org/woop-1.

[32] Motivation is the central focus of the self-determination theory, which examines the interplay between external motivation and internal motivation. It highlights competence, autonomy, and relatedness as critical for internal motivation. In our experience, those factors are at the core of purpose as well. Learn more about the self-determination theory at www.selfdeterminationtheory.org/theory.

[33] Dr. Deborah Stipek and Kathy Seal discuss positive reinforcement in their book *Motivated Minds: Raising Children to Love Learning*.

[34] Edward M. Hallowell is the founder of Hallowell Center, a mental health center that specializes in treating ADHD. Learn more at www.hallowellnyc.com.

35 Our articulation of the coach approach is based on our own teaching and coaching experience and the core components of life coach training. More information about coaching is available at www.ipeccoaching.com.

36 In his 2002 book *The Childhood Roots of Adult Happiness*, psychiatrist Edward M. Hallowell describes the importance of connection, play, practice, mastery, and recognition.

37 For more information on the effective implementation of to-do lists, Atul Gawande's *The Checklist Manifesto* comprises real-life stories of checklists helping to manage the complexity of modern life.

38 Fernando Gómez-Pinilla's article "Brain Foods: The Effects of Nutrients on Brain Function" discusses the impact of diet on brain health and mental function.

39 Benjamin Sibley and Jennifer Etnier research the relationship between physical activity and cognition in children in their 2003 article "The Relationship between Physical Activity and Cognition in Children."

40 See Julia Dewald-Kaufmann and her team's article "The Influence of Sleep Quality, Sleep Duration, and Sleepiness on School Performance in Children and Adolescents."

41 Stephanie Sutherland discusses the effects of screens on melatonin production in her article "Bright Screens Could Delay Bedtime" at www.scientificamerican.com/article/bright-screens-could-delay-bedtime.

42 Learn more at www.mindfulschools.org.

43 James M. Lang explores small changes teachers can make in the classroom that will support effective, deep, and durable learning in his 2016 book *Small Teaching*.

44 The Learning Toolbox includes specific directions for students, teachers, and parents at coe.jmu.edu/learningtoolbox/cornellnotes.html.

45 The Pretest Self-Reflection worksheet is adapted from work created by Cecilia Bonnabeau, a math teacher at Riverdale Country School. The Error Analysis for Math worksheet is adapted from work created by Kyle Davidson, a math teacher at Horace Mann School.

46 Classroom exercises are adapted from the Mindful Schools' "Educator Essentials" online professional development course at www.mindfulschools.org.

REFERENCES

Barkley, R. A. (2000). *Taking charge of ADHD: The complete, authoritative guide for parents.* New York: Guilford Press.

Benson, H., & Klipper, M. (2000). *The relaxation response.* New York: HarperTorch

Brown, P., Roediger III, H., & McDaniel, M. (2014). *Make it stick: The science of successful learning.* Cambridge, MA: Belknap Press.

Bunce, D. M., Flens, E. A., & Neiles, K. Y. (2010). How long can students pay attention in class? A study of student attention decline using clickers. *Journal of Chemical Education, 87*(12), 1438–1443. doi:10.1021/ed100409p

Character Lab. (n.d.). Retrieved May 23, 2017, from https://characterlab.org/

Dawson, P., & Guare, R. (2009). *Smart but scattered: The revolutionary "executive skills" approach to helping kids reach their potential.* New York: Guilford Press.

Deak, J. (2010). *How girls thrive.* Columbus, OH: Green Blanket Press.

Dewald, J. F., Meijer, A. M., Oort, F. J., Kerkhof, G. A., & Bögels, S. M. (2010). The influence of sleep quality, sleep duration, and sleepiness on school performance in children and adolescents: A meta-analytic review. *Sleep Medicine Reviews, 14*(3), 179–189. doi:10.1016/j.smrv.2009.10.004

Diamond, A. (2013). Executive Functions. *Annual Review of Psychology, 64*(1), 135-168. doi:10.1146/annurev-psych-113011-14375

Dunlosky, J. (2013). Strengthening the student toolbox: Study strategies to boost learning. *American Educator, 37*(3), 12–21.

Dweck, C. (2016). *Mindset: The new psychology of success.* New York: Ballantine Books.

Dweck, C. (2016, January 11). Recognizing and overcoming false growth mindset. *Edutopia.* Retrieved from www.edutopia.org/blog/recognizing-overcoming-false-growth-mindset-carol-dweck

Gawande, Atul. (2011). *The checklist manifesto: How to get things right.* New York: Picador.

Goleman, D. (2005). *Emotional intelligence: Why it can matter more than IQ*. New York: Bantam Books.

Gómez-Pinilla, F. (2008). Brain foods: The effects of nutrients on brain function. *Nature Reviews Neuroscience, 9*(7), 568–578. doi:10.1038/nrn2421

Hallowell, E.M. (2002). *The childhood roots of adult happiness: Five steps to help kids create and sustain lifelong joy.* New York: Ballantine.

Lang, J.M (2016) *Small teaching: Everyday lessons from the science of learning.* San Francisco, CA: Jossey-Bass

Langer, E. (1997). *The power of mindful learning.* Cambridge, MA: Da Capo Press.

Meltzer, L. (2010). *Promoting executive function in the classroom (what works for special-needs learners.* New York: Guilford Press.

Mindful Schools. (n.d.). Retrieved May 23, 2017, from http://www.mindfulschools.org/

Oettingen, G. (2015). *Rethinking positive thinking: Inside the new science of motivation.* New York: Current.

Rubinstein, J. S., Meyer, D. E., & Evans, J. E. (2001). Executive control of cognitive processes in task switching. *Journal of Experimental Psychology, 27*(4), 763–797. dx.doi.org/10.1037/0096-1523.27.4.763

Sibley, B. A., & Etnier, J. L. (2003). The Relationship between Physical Activity and Cognition in Children: A Meta-Analysis. *Pediatric Exercise Science, 15*(3), 243-256. doi:10.1123/pes.15.3.243

Steinberg, L. (2008). A social neuroscience perspective on adolescent risk-taking. *Developmental Review, 28*(1), 78–106. doi:10.1016/j.dr.2007.08.002

Steinberg, L. (2015). *Age of opportunity.* New York: First Mariner Books.

Stipek, D., & Seal, K. (2001). *Motivated minds: Raising children to love learning.* New York: Henry Holt.

Sutherland, S. (2012). Bright Screens Could Delay Bedtime. *Scientific American Mind, 23*(6), 13-13. doi:10.1038/scientificamericanmind0113-13b

The Learning Toolbox - Cornell Notes. (n.d.). Retrieved May 23, 2017, from http://coe.jmu.edu/learningtoolbox/cornellnotes.htm

Weinschenk, S. (2012, September 18). The true cost of multi-tasking. [Web log post]. Retrieved from www.psychologytoday.com/blog/brain-wise/201209/the-true-cost-multi-tasking

Willingham, D. T. (2009). *Why don't students like school?: A cognitive scientist answers questions about how the mind works and what it means for the classroom.* San Francisco: Jossey-Bass.

Yeager, D., Walton, G., & Cohen, G. L. (2013). Addressing achievement gaps with psychological interventions. *Phi Delta Kappan, 94*(5), 62–65. doi: 10.1177/003172171309400514

Zenner, C., Herrnleben-Kurz, S., & Walach, H. (2014). Mindfulness-based interventions in schools—a systematic review and meta-analysis. *Frontiers in Psychology, 5,* 603. doi:10.3389/fpsyg.2014.00603

Online Resources

American Psychological Association—www.apa.org

Character Lab—www.characterlab.org

Development Cognitive Neuroscience Lab of Adele Diamond—www.devcogneuro.com

Mindful Schools—www.mindfulschools.org

Self-Determination Theory—www.selfdeterminationtheory.org/theory

Hallowell Center—hallowellnyc.com

iPEC Coach Training—www.ipeccoaching.com

Learning Toolbox—coe.jmu.edu/learningtoolbox/cornellnotes.html

VIA Institute on Character—www.viacharacter.org

WOOP Mental Contrasting—woopmylife.org/woop-1

ABOUT THE AUTHOR

Christina Young, M.S.Ed., LPC, is a licensed mental health and school counselor. She draws on 15 years of experience as a counselor, life coach, yoga and mindfulness teacher, classroom teacher, and learning specialist to help individuals and organizations strengthen performance while improving mindfulness and overall wellbeing. As director of student life, she facilitates and develops health and wellbeing programs at the leading independent Riverdale Country School. Christina is also a learning designer at the educational consultancy Plussed and a life coach at Hallowell Center.

CONTRIBUTORS

Christina Nichols, Ph.D., is a licensed clinical psychologist with extensive experience helping individuals with anxiety, neurological, and learning differences. She is middle school psychologist at the leading independent Horace Mann School and a therapist at Hallowell Center. She incorporates her extensive experience in psychology, education, and neuroscience in her work with adolescents and adults, identifying areas of strength and improving performance and overall wellbeing.

Edward Hallowell, M.D., is a child and adult psychiatrist, a *New York Times* best-selling author, a world-renowned speaker, and a leading authority in the field of ADHD. He is the founder of Hallowell Centers in Boston, MetroWest, New York City, San Francisco, and Seattle. He was a Harvard Medical School faculty member for 21 years and now devotes his full professional attention to his clinical practice, lectures, and the writing of books, including *Driven to Distraction* and *The Childhood Roots of Adult Happiness*.

CPSIA information can be obtained at www.ICGtesting.com
Printed in the USA
BVIW12n2339120617
486717BV00002B/3